AMONG THE MEADOW PEOPLE

Look for these other great books by Clara Dillingham
Pierson also from Living Book Press

- Among the Farmyard People
- Among the Pond People
- Among the Forest People
- Among the Meadow People
- Among the Night People
- Dooryard Stories
- Tales from a Poultry Farm

WWW.LIVINGBOOKPRESS.COM

This edition published 2021
by Living Book Press
Copyright © Living Book Press, 2021

ISBN: 978-1-922634-24-5 (hardcover)
        978-1-922634-23-8 (softcover)

First published in 1899.

A catalogue record for this
book is available from the
National Library of Australia

Among the Meadow People

BY

CLARA DILLINGHAM PIERSON

LIVING BOOK
PRESS

CONTENTS

INTRODUCTION.

Many of these stories of field life were written for the little ones of my kindergarten, and they gave so much pleasure, and aroused such a new interest in "the meadow people," that it has seemed wise to collect and add to the original number and send them out to a larger circle of boys and girls.

All mothers and teachers hear the cry for "just one more," and find that there are times when the bewitching tales of animals, fairies, and "really truly" children are all exhausted, and tired imagination will not supply another. In selecting the tiny creatures of field and garden for the characters in this book, I have remembered with pleasure the way in which my loyal pupils befriended stray crickets and grasshoppers, their intense appreciation of the new realm of fancy and observation, and the eagerness and attention with which they sought Mother Nature, the most wonderful and tireless of all story-tellers.

Clara Dillingham Pierson.
STANTON, MICHIGAN, *April 8th, 1897.*

The BUTTERFLY That WENT CALLING

As the warm August days came, Mr. Yellow Butterfly wriggled and pushed in his snug little green chrysalis and wished he could get out to see the world. He remembered the days when he was a hairy little Caterpillar, crawling slowly over grass and leaves, and he remembered how beautiful the sky and all the flowers were. Then he thought of the new wings which had been growing from his back, and he tried to move them, just to see how it would feel. He had only six legs since his wings grew, and he missed all the sticky feet which he had to give up when he began to change into a Butterfly.

The more he thought about it the more he squirmed, until suddenly he heard a faint little sound, too faint for larger people to

hear, and found a tiny slit in the wall of his chrysalis. It was such a dainty green chrysalis with white wrinkles, that it seemed almost a pity to have it break. Still it had held him for eight days already and that was as long as any of his family ever hung in the chrysalis, so it was quite time for it to be torn open and left empty. Mr. Yellow Butterfly belonged to the second brood that had hatched that year and he wanted to be out while the days were still fine and hot. Now he crawled out of the newly-opened doorway to take his first flight.

Poor Mr. Butterfly! He found his wings so wet and crinkled that they wouldn't work at all, so he had to sit quietly in the sunshine all day drying them. And just as they got big, and smooth, and dry, it grew dark, and Mr. Butterfly had to crawl under a leaf to sleep.

The next morning, bright and early, he flew away to visit the flowers. First he stopped to see the Daisies by the roadside. They were all dancing in the wind, and their bright faces looked as cheerful as anyone could wish. They were glad to see Mr. Butterfly, and wished him to stay all day with them. He said; "You are very kind, but I really couldn't think of doing it. You must excuse my saying it, but I am surprised to think you will grow here. It is very dusty and dry, and then there is no shade. I am sure I could have chosen a better place."

The Daisies smiled and nodded to each other, saying, "This is the kind of place we were made for, that's all."

Mr. Butterfly shook his head very doubtfully, and then bade them a polite "Good-morning," and flew away to call on the Cardinals.

The Cardinals are a very stately family, as everybody knows. They hold their heads very high, and never make deep bows, even to the wind, but for all that they are a very pleasant family to meet. They gave Mr. Butterfly a dainty lunch of honey, and seemed much pleased when he told them how beautiful the river looked in the sunlight.

"It is a delightful place to grow," said they.

"Ye-es," said Mr. Butterfly, "it is very pretty, still I do not think it can be healthful. I really cannot understand why you flowers choose such strange homes. Now, there are the Daisies, where I just called. They are in a dusty, dry place, where there is no shade at all. I spoke to them about it, and they acted quite uppish."

"But the Daisies always do choose such places," said the Cardinals.

"And your family," said Mr. Butterfly, "have lived so long in wet places that it is a wonder you are alive. Your color is good, but to stand with one's roots in water all the time! It is shocking."

"Cardinals and Butterflies live differently," said the flowers. "Good-morning."

Mr. Butterfly left the river and flew over to the woods. He was very much out of patience. He was so angry that his feelers quivered, and now you know how angry he must have been. He knew that the Violets were a very agreeable family, who never put on airs, so he went at once to them.

He had barely said "Good-morning" to them when he began to explain what had displeased him.

"To think," he said, "what notions some flowers have! Now, you have a pleasant home here in the edge of the woods. I have been telling the Daisies and the Cardinals that they should grow in such a place, but they wouldn't listen to me. The Daisies were quite uppish about it, and the Cardinals were very stiff."

"My dear friend," answered a Violet, "they could never live if they moved up into our neighborhood. Every flower has his own place in this world, and is happiest in that place. Everything has its own place and its own work, and every flower that is wise will stay in the place for which it was intended. You were exceedingly kind to want to help the flowers, but suppose they had been telling you what to do. Suppose the Cardinals had told you that flying around was not good for your health, and that to be truly well you ought to grow planted with your legs in the mud and water."

"Oh!" said Mr. Butterfly, "Oh! I never thought of that. Perhaps Butterflies don't know everything."

"No," said the Violet, "they don't know everything, and you haven't been out of your chrysalis very long. But those who are ready to learn can always find someone to tell them. Won't you eat some honey?"

And Mr. Butterfly sipped honey and was happy.

THE ROBINS
BUILD A NEST.

WHEN Mr. and Mrs. Robin built in the spring, they were not quite agreed as to where the nest should be. Mr. Robin was a very decided bird, and had made up his mind that the lowest crotch of a maple tree would be the best place. He even went so far as to take three billfuls of mud there, and stick in two blades of dry grass. Mrs. Robin wanted it on the end of the second rail from the top of the split-rail fence. She said it was high enough from the ground to be safe and dry, and not so high that a little bird falling out of it would hurt himself very much. Then, too, the top rail was broad at the end and would keep the rain off so well.

"And the nest will be just the color of the rails," said she, "so that even a Red Squirrel could hardly see it." She disliked Red Squirrels, and she had reason to, for she had been married before, and if it had not been for a Red Squirrel, she might already have had children as large as she was.

"I say that the tree is the place for it," said Mr. Robin, "and I wear the brightest breast feathers." He said this because in bird families the one who wears the brightest breast feathers thinks he has the right to decide things.

Mrs. Robin was wise enough not to answer back when he spoke in this way. She only shook her feathers, took ten quick running steps, tilted her body forward, looked hard at the ground, and pulled out something for supper. After that she fluttered around the maple tree crotch as though she had never thought of any other place. Mr. Robin wished he had not been quite so decided, or reminded her of his breast feathers. "After all," thought he, "I don't know but the fence-rail would have done." He thought this, but he didn't say it. It is not always easy for a Robin to give up and let one with dull breast feathers know that he thinks himself wrong.

That night they perched in the maple-tree and slept with their heads under their wings. Long before the sun was in sight, when the first beams were just touching the tops of the forest trees, they awakened, bright-eyed and rested, preened their feathers, sang their morning song, "Cheerily, cheerily, cheer-up," and flew off to find food. After breakfast they began to work on the nest. Mrs. Robin stopped often to look and peck at the bark. "It will take a great deal of mud," said she, "to fill in that deep crotch until we reach a place wide enough for the nest."

At another time she said: "My dear, I am afraid that the dry grass you are bringing is too light-colored. It shows very plainly against the maple bark. Can't you find some that is darker?"

Mr. Robin hunted and hunted, but could find nothing which was darker. As he flew past the fence, he noticed that it was almost the color of the grass in his bill.

After a while, soft gray clouds began to cover the sky. "I wonder," said Mrs. Robin, "if it will rain before we get this done. The mud is soft enough now to work well, and this place is so open that the rain might easily wash away all that we have done."

It did rain, however, and very soon. The great drops came down so hard that one could only think of pebbles falling. Mr. and Mrs. Robin oiled their feathers as quickly as they could, taking the oil from their back pockets and putting it onto their feathers with their bills. This made the finest kind of waterproof and was not at all heavy to wear. When the rain was over they shook themselves and looked at their work.

"I believe," said Mrs. Robin to her husband, "that you are right in saying that we might better give up this place and begin over again somewhere else."

Now Mr. Robin could not remember having said that he thought anything of the sort, and he looked very sharply at his wife, and cocked his black head on one side until all the black and white streaks on his throat showed. She did not seem to know that he was watching her as she hopped around the partly built nest, poking it here and pushing it there, and trying her hardest to make it look right. He thought she would say something, but she didn't. Then he knew he must speak first. He flirted his tail and tipped his head and drew some of his brown wing-feathers through his bill. Then he held himself very straight and tall, and said, "Well, if you do agree with me, I think you might much better stop working here and begin in another place."

"It seems almost too bad," said she. "Of course there are other places, but—"

By this time Mr. Robin knew exactly what to do. "Plenty of them," said he. "Now don't fuss any longer with this. That place on the rail fence is an excellent one. I wonder that no other birds have taken it." As he spoke he flew ahead to the very spot which Mrs. Robin had first chosen.

She was a very wise bird, and knew far too much to say, "I told you so." Saying that, you know, always makes things go wrong. She looked at the rail fence, ran along the top of it, toeing in prettily as she ran, looked around in a surprised way, and said, "Oh, *that* place?"

"Yes, Mrs. Robin," said her husband, "*that* place. Do you see anything wrong about it?"

"No-o," she said. "I think I could make it do."

Before long another nest was half built, and Mrs. Robin was working away in the happiest manner possible, stopping every little while to sing her afternoon song: "Do you think what you do? Do you think what you do? Do you thi-ink?"

Mr. Robin was also at work, and such billfuls of mud, such fine little twigs, and such big wisps of dry grass as went into that home! Once Mr. Robin was gone a long time, and when he came back he had a beautiful piece of white cotton string dangling from his beak. That they put on the outside. "Not that we care to show off," said they, "but somehow that seemed to be the best place to put it."

Mr. Robin was very proud of his nest and of his wife. He never went far away if he could help it. Once she heard him tell Mr. Goldfinch that, "Mrs. Robin was very sweet about building where he chose, and that even after he insisted on changing places from the tree to the fence she was perfectly good-natured."

"Yes," said Mrs. Robin to Mrs. Goldfinch, "I was perfectly good-natured." Then she gave a happy, chirpy little laugh, and Mrs. Goldfinch laughed, too. They were perfectly contented birds, even if they didn't wear the brightest breast feathers or insist on having their own way. And Mrs. Robin had been married before.

THE SELFISH TENT-CATERPILLAR.

ONE could hardly call the Tent-Caterpillars meadow people, for they did not often leave their trees to crawl upon the ground. Yet the Apple-Tree Tent-Caterpillars would not allow anybody to call them forest people. "We live on apple and wild cherry trees," they said, "and you will almost always find us in the orchards or on the roadside trees. There are Forest Tent-Caterpillars, but please don't get us mixed with them. We belong to another branch of the family, the Apple-Tree branch."

The Tree Frog said that he remembered perfectly well when the eggs were laid on the wild cherry tree on the edge of the meadow. "It was early last summer," he said, "and the Moth who laid them was a very agreeable reddish-brown person, about as large as a common Yellow Butterfly. I remember that she had two light yellow lines on each fore-wing. Another Moth came with her, but did not stay. He was smaller than she, and had the same markings. After he had gone, she asked me if we were ever visited by the Yellow-Billed Cuckoos."

"Why did she ask that?" said the Garter Snake.

"Don't you know?" exclaimed the Tree Frog. And then he whispered something to the Garter Snake.

The Garter Snake wriggled with surprise and cried, "Really?"

All through the fall and winter the many, many eggs which the reddish-brown Moth had laid were kept snug and warm on the twig where she had put them. They were placed in rows around the twig, and then well covered to hold them together and keep them warm. The winter winds had blown the twig to and fro, the cold rain had frozen over them, the soft snowflakes had drifted down from the clouds and covered them, only to melt and trickle away again in shining drops. One morning the whole wild cherry tree was covered with beautiful long, glistening crystals of hoar-frost; and still the ring of eggs stayed in its place around the twig, and the life in them slept until spring sunbeams should shine down and quicken it.

But when the spring sunbeams did come! Even before the leaf-buds were open, tiny Larvæ, or Caterpillar babies, came crawling from the ring of eggs and began feeding upon the buds. They took very, very small bites, and that looked as though they were polite children. Still, you know, their mouths were so small that they could not take big ones, and it may not have been politeness after all which made them eat daintily.

When all the Tent-Caterpillars were hatched, and they had eaten every leaf-bud near the egg-ring, they began to crawl down the tree toward the trunk. Once they stopped by a good-sized crotch in the branches. "Let's build here," said the leader; "this place is all right."

Then some of the Tent-Caterpillars said, "Let's!" and some of them said, "Don't let's!" One young fellow said, "Aw, come on! There's a bigger crotch farther down." Of course he should have said, "I think you will like a larger crotch better," but he was young, and, you know, these Larvæ had no father or mother to help them speak in the right way. They were orphans, and it is wonderful how they ever learned to talk at all.

After this, some of the Tent-Caterpillars went on to the larger crotch and some stayed behind. More went than stayed, and when they saw this, those by the smaller crotch gave up and joined their brothers and sisters, as they should have done. It was right to do that which pleased most of them.

It took a great deal of work to make the tent. All helped, spinning hundreds and thousands of white silken threads, laying them side by side, criss-crossing them, fastening the ends to branches and twigs, not forgetting to leave places through which one could crawl in and out. They never worked all day at this, because unless they stopped to eat they would soon have been weak and unable to spin. There were nearly always a few Caterpillars in the tent, but only in the early morning or late afternoon or during the night were they all at home. The rest of the time they were scattered around the tree feeding. Of course there were some cold days when they stayed in. When the weather was chilly they moved slowly and cared very little for food.

There was one young Tent-Caterpillar who happened to be the first hatched, and who seemed to think that because he was a minute older than any of the other children he had the right to his own way. Sometimes he got it, because the others didn't want to have any trouble. Sometimes he didn't get it, and then he was very sulky and disagreeable, even refusing to answer when he was spoken to.

One cold day, when all the Caterpillars stayed in the tent, this oldest brother wanted the warmest place, that in the very middle. It should have belonged to the younger brothers and sisters, for they were not so strong, but he pushed and wriggled his hairy black and brown and yellow body into the very place he wanted, and then scolded everybody around because he had to push to get there. It happened as it always does when a Caterpillar begins to say mean things, and he went on until he was saying some which were really untrue. Nobody answered back, so he scolded and fussed and was exceedingly disagreeable.

All day long he thought how wretched he was, and how badly they treated him, and how he guessed they'd be sorry enough if he went away. The next morning he went. As long as the warm sunshine lasted he did very well. When it began to grow cool, his brothers and sisters crawled past him on their way to the tent. "Come on!" they cried. "It's time to go home."

"Uh-uh!" said the eldest brother (and that meant "No"), "I'm not going."

"Why not?" they asked.

"Oh, because," said he.

When the rest were all together in the tent they talked about him. "Do you suppose he's angry?" said one.

"What should he be angry about?" said another.

"I just believe he is," said a third. "Did you notice the way his hairs bristled?"

"Don't you think we ought to go to get him?" asked two or three of the youngest Caterpillars.

"No," said the older ones. "We haven't done anything. Let him get over it."

So the oldest brother, who had thought that every other

Caterpillar in the tent would crawl right out and beg and coax him to come back, waited and waited and waited, but nobody came. The tent was there and the door was open. All he had to do was to crawl in and be at home. He waited so long that at last he had to leave the tree and spin his cocoon without ever having gone back to his brothers and sisters in the tent. He spun his cocoon and mixed the silk with a yellowish-white powder, then he lay down in it to sleep twenty-one days and grow his wings. The last thought he had before going to sleep was an unhappy and selfish one. Probably he awakened an unhappy and selfish Moth.

His brothers and sisters were sad whenever they thought of him. But, they said, "what could we do? It wasn't fair for him to have the best of everything, and we never answered when he said mean things. He might have come back at any time and we would have been kind to him."

And they were right. What could they have done? It was very sad, but when a Caterpillar is so selfish and sulky that he cannot live happily with other people, it is much better that he should live quite alone.

THE LAZY SNAIL

In the lower part of the meadow, where the grass grew tall and tender, there lived a fine and sturdy young Snail; that is to say, a fine-looking Snail. His shell was a beautiful soft gray, and its curves were regular and perfect. His body was soft and moist, and just what a Snail's body should be. Of course, when it came to travelling, he could not go fast, for none of his family are rapid travellers, still, if he had been plucky and patient, he might have seen much of the meadow, and perhaps some of the world outside. His friends and neighbors often told him that he ought to start out on a little journey to see the sights, but he would always answer, "Oh, it is too hard work!"

There was nobody who liked stories of

16

meadow life better than this same Snail, and he would often stop some friendly Cricket or Snake to ask for the news. After they had told him, they would say, "Why, don't you ever get out to see these things for yourself?" and he would give a little sigh and answer, "It is too far to go."

"But you needn't go the whole distance in one day," his visitor would say, "only a little at a time."

"Yes, and then I would have to keep starting on again every little while," the Snail would reply. "What of that?" said the visitor; "you would have plenty of resting spells, when you could lie in the shade of a tall weed and enjoy yourself."

"Well, what is the use?" the Snail would say. "I can't enjoy resting if I know I've got to go to work again," and he would sigh once more.

So there he lived, eating and sleeping, and wishing he could see the world, and meet the people in the upper part of the meadow, but just so lazy that he wouldn't start out to find them.

He never thought that the Butterflies and Beetles might not like it to have him keep calling them to him and making them tell him the news. Oh, no indeed! If he wanted them to do anything for him, he asked them quickly enough, and they, being happy, good-natured people, would always do as he asked them to.

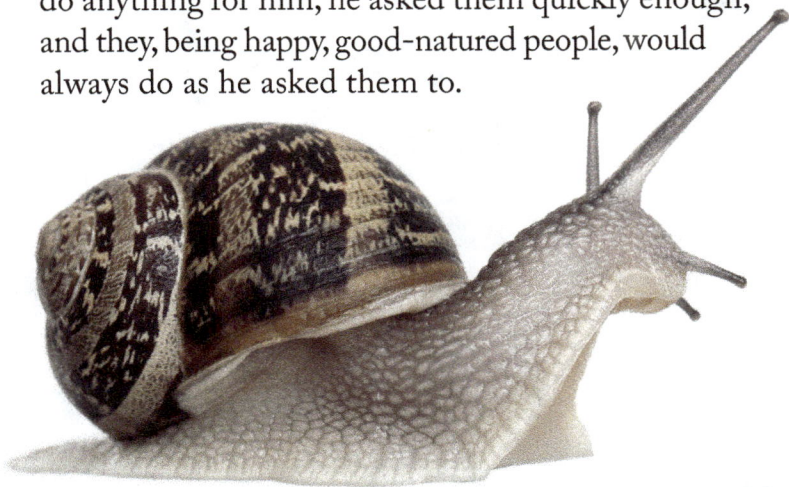

There came a day, though, when he asked too much. The Grasshoppers had been telling him about some very delicious new plants that grew a little distance away, and the Snail wanted some very badly. "Can't you bring me some?" he said. "There are so many of you, and you have such good, strong legs. I should think you might each bring me a small piece in your mouths, and then I should have a fine dinner of it."

The Grasshoppers didn't say anything then, but when they were so far away that he could not hear them, they said to each other, "If the Snail wants the food so much, he might better go for it. We have other things to do," and they hopped off on their own business.

The Snail sat there, and wondered and wondered that they did not come. He kept thinking how he would like some of the new food for dinner, but there it ended. He didn't want it enough to get it for himself.

The Grasshoppers told all their friends about the Snail's request, and everybody thought, "Such a lazy, good-for-nothing fellow deserves to be left quite alone." So it happened that for a very long time nobody went near the Snail.

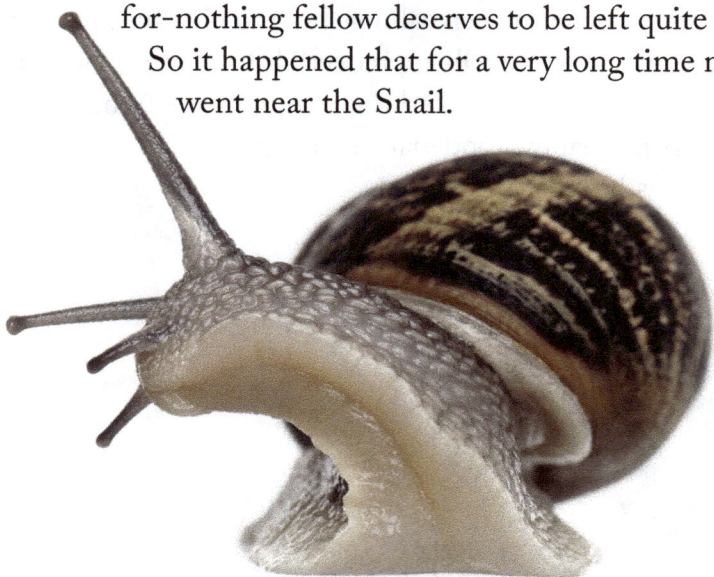

The weather grew hotter and hotter. The clouds, which blew across the sky, kept their rain until they were well past the meadow, and so it happened that the river grew shallower and shallower, and the sunshine dried the tiny pools and rivulets which kept the lower meadow damp. The grass began to turn brown and dry, and, all in all, it was trying weather for Snails.

One day, a Butterfly called some of her friends together, and told them that she had seen the Snail lying in his old place, looking thin and hungry. "The grass is all dried around him," she said; "I believe he is starving, and too lazy to go nearer the river, where there is still good food for him."

They all talked it over together, and some of them said it was of no use to help a Snail who was too lazy to do anything for himself. Others said, "Well, he is too weak to help himself now, at all events, and we might help him this once." And that is exactly what they did. The Butterflies and the Mosquitoes flew ahead to find the best place to put the Snail, and all the Grasshoppers, and Beetles, and other strong crawling creatures took turns in rolling the Snail down toward the river.

They left him where the green things were fresh and tender, and he grew strong and plump once more. It is even said that he was not so lazy afterward, but one cannot tell whether to believe it or not, for everybody knows that when people let themselves grow up lazy, as he did, it is almost impossible for them to get over it when they want to. One thing is sure: the meadow people who helped him were happier and better for doing a kind thing, no matter what became of the Snail.

THE ANT THAT WORE WINGS

In one of the Ant-hills in the highest part of the meadow, were a lot of young Ants talking together. "I," said one, "am going to be a soldier, and drive away anybody who comes to make us trouble. I try biting hard things every day to make my jaws strong, so that I can guard the home better."

"I," said another and smaller Ant, "want to be a worker. I want to help build and repair the home. I want to get the food for the family, and feed the Ant babies, and clean them off when they crawl out of their old coats. If I can do those things well, I shall be the happiest, busiest Ant in the meadow."

"We don't want to live that kind of life," said a couple of larger Ants with wings. "We don't mean to stay around the Ant-hill all the time and work. We want to use our wings, and then you may be very sure that you won't see us around home any more."

The little worker spoke up: "Home is a

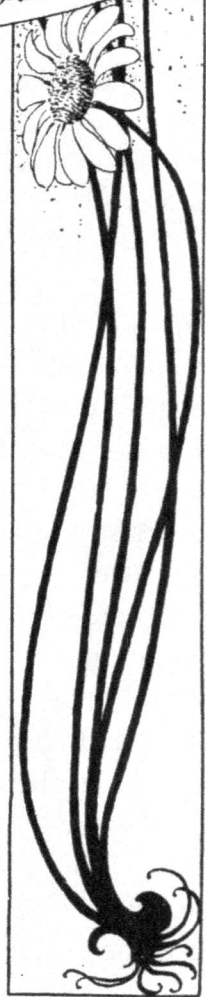

pleasant place. You may be very glad to come back to it some day." But the Ants with the wings turned their backs and wouldn't listen to another word.

A few days after this there were exciting times in the Ant-hill. All the winged Ants said "Good-bye" to the soldiers and workers, and flew off through the air, flew so far that the little ones at home could no longer see them. All day long they were gone, but the next morning when the little worker (whom we heard talking) went out to get breakfast, she found the poor winged Ants lying on the ground near their home. Some of them were dead, and the rest were looking for food.

The worker Ant ran up to the one who had said she didn't want to stay around home, and asked her to come back to the Ant-hill. "No, I thank you," she answered. "I have had my breakfast now, and am going to fly off again." She raised her wings to go, but after she had given one flutter, they dropped off, and she could never fly again.

The worker hurried back to the Ant-hill to call some of her sister workers, and some of the soldiers, and they took the Ant who had lost her wings and carried her to another part of the meadow. There they went to work to build a new home and make her their queen.

First, they looked for a good, sandy place, on which the sun would shine all day. Then the worker Ants began to dig in the ground and bring out tiny round pieces of earth in their mouths. The soldiers helped them, and before night they had a cosy little home in the earth, with several rooms, and some food already stored. They took their queen in, and brought her food to eat, and waited on her, and she was happy and contented.

By and by the Ant eggs began to hatch, and the workers had all they could do to take care of their queen and her little Ant babies, and the soldier Ants had to help. The Ant babies were little worms or grubs when they first came out of the eggs; after a while they curled up in tiny, tiny cases, called pupa-cases, and after another while they came out of these, and then they looked like the older Ants, with their six legs, and their slender little waists. But whatever they were, whether eggs, or grubs, or curled up in the pupa-cases, or lively little Ants, the workers fed and took care of them, and the soldiers fought for them, and the queen-mother loved them, and they all lived happily together until the young Ants were ready to go out into the great world and learn the lessons of life for themselves.

THE CHEERFUL HARVESTMEN

SOME of the meadow people are gay and careless, and some are always worrying. Some work hard every day, and some are exceedingly lazy. There, as everywhere else, each has his own way of thinking about things. It is too bad that they cannot all learn to think brave and cheerful thoughts, for these make life happy. One may have a comfortable home, kind neighbors, and plenty to eat, yet if he is in the habit of thinking disagreeable thoughts, not even all these good things can make him happy. Now there was the young Frog who thought herself sick—but that is another story.

Perhaps the Harvestmen were the most cheerful of all the meadow people. The old Tree Frog used to say that it made him feel better just to see their knees coming toward him. Of course, when he saw their knees, he knew that the whole insect was also coming. He spoke in that way because the Harvestmen always walked or ran with their knees so much above the rest of their bodies that one could see those first.

The Harvestmen were not particularly fine-looking, not nearly so handsome as some of their Spider cousins. One never thought of that, however. They had such an easy way of moving around on their eight legs, each of which had a great many joints. It is the joints, or bending-places, you know, which make legs useful. Besides being graceful, they had very pleasant manners. When a Harvestman said "Good-morning" to you on a rainy day, you always had a feeling that the sun was shining. It might be that the drops were even then falling into your face, but for a moment you were sure to feel that everything was bright and warm and comfortable.

Sometimes the careless young Grasshoppers and Crickets called the Harvestmen by their nicknames, "Daddy Long-Legs" or "Grandfather Graybeard." Even then the Harvestmen were good-natured, and only said with a smile that the young people had not yet learned the names of their neighbors. The Grasshoppers never seemed to think how queer it was to call a young Harvestman daughter "Grandfather Graybeard." When they saw how good-natured they were, the Grasshoppers soon stopped trying to tease the Harvestmen. People who are really good-natured are never teased very long, you know.

The Walking-Sticks were exceedingly polite to the Harvestmen. They thought them very slender and genteel-looking. Once the Five-Legged Walking-Stick said to the largest Harvestman, "Why do you talk so much with the common people in the meadow?"

The Harvestman knew exactly what the Walking-Stick meant, but he was not going to let anybody make fun of his

kind and friendly neighbors, so he said: "I think we Harvestmen are rather common ourselves. There are a great, great many of us here. It must be very lonely to be uncommon."

After that the Walking-Stick had nothing more to say. He never felt quite sure whether the Harvestman was too stupid to understand or too wise to gossip. Once he thought he saw the Harvestman's eyes twinkle. The Harvestman didn't care if people thought him stupid. He knew that he was not stupid, and he would rather seem dull than to listen while unkind things were said about his neighbors.

Some people would have thought it very hard luck to be Harvestmen. The Garter Snake said that if he were one, he should be worried all the time about his legs. "I'm thankful I haven't any," he said, "for if I had I should be forever thinking I should lose some of them. A Harvestman without legs would be badly off. He could never in the world crawl around on his belly as I do."

How the Harvestmen did laugh when they heard this! The biggest one said, "Well, if that isn't just like some people! Never want to have anything for fear they'll lose it. I wonder if he worries about his head? He might lose that, you know, and then what would he do?"

It was only the next day that the largest Harvestman came home on seven legs. His friends all cried out, "Oh, how did it ever happen?"

"Cows," said he.

"Did they step on you?" asked the Five-Legged Walking-Stick. He had not lived long enough in the meadow to understand all that the Harvestman meant. He was sorry for him, though, for he knew what it was to lose a leg.

"Huh!" said a Grasshopper, interrupting in a very rude way, "aren't any Cows in this meadow now!"

Then the other Harvestmen told the Walking-Stick all about it, how sometimes a boy would come to the meadow, catch a Harvestman, hold him up by one leg, and say to him, "Grandfather Graybeard, tell me where the Cows are, or I'll kill you." Then the only thing a Harvestman could do was to struggle and wriggle himself free, and he often broke off a leg in doing so.

"How terrible!" said the three Walking-Sticks all together. "But why don't you tell them?"

"We do," answered the Harvestmen. "We point with our seven other legs, and we point every way there is. Sometimes we don't know where they are, so we point everywhere, to be sure. But it doesn't make any difference. Our legs drop off just the same."

"Isn't a boy clever enough to find Cows alone?" asked the Walking-Sticks.

"Oh, it isn't that," cried all the meadow people together. "Even after you tell, and sometimes when the Cows are right there, they walk off home without them."

"I'd sting them," said a Wasp, waving his feelers fiercely and raising and lowering his wings. "I'd sting them as hard as I could."

"You wouldn't if you had no sting," said the Tree Frog.

"N-no," stammered the Wasp, "I suppose I wouldn't."

"You poor creature!" said the biggest Katydid to the biggest Harvestman. "What will you do? Only seven legs!"

"Do?" answered the biggest Harvestman, and it was then one could see how truly brave and cheerful he was. "Do?

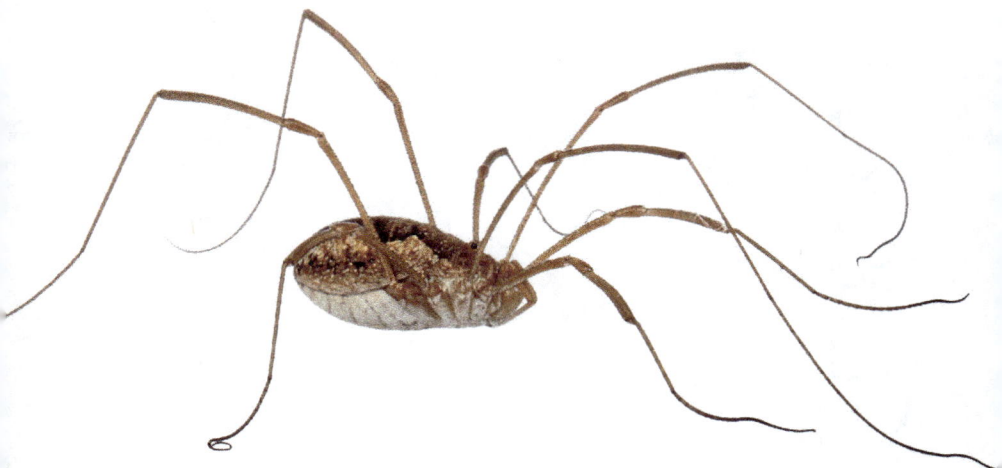

I'll walk on those seven. If I lose one of them I'll walk on six, and if I lose one of them I'll walk on five. Haven't I my mouth and my stomach and my eyes and my two feelers, and my two food-pincers? I may not be so good-looking, but I am a Harvestman, and I shall enjoy the grass and the sunshine and my kind neighbors as long as I live. I must leave you now. Good-day."

He walked off rather awkwardly, for he had not yet learned to manage himself since his accident. The meadow people looked after him very thoughtfully. They were not noticing his awkwardness, or thinking of his high knees or of his little low body. Perhaps they thought what the Cicada said, "Ah, that is the way to live!"

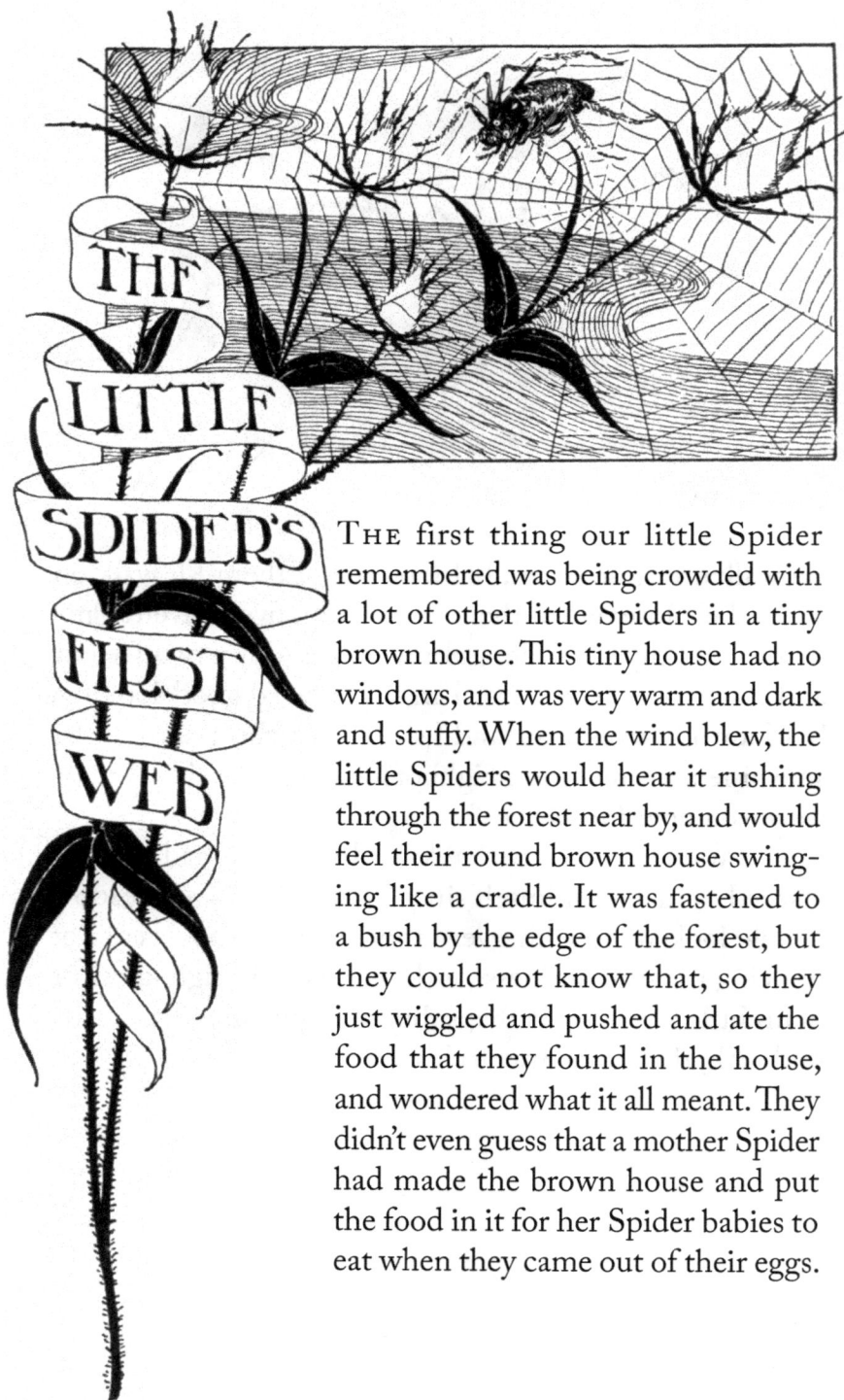

THE LITTLE SPIDER'S FIRST WEB

THE first thing our little Spider remembered was being crowded with a lot of other little Spiders in a tiny brown house. This tiny house had no windows, and was very warm and dark and stuffy. When the wind blew, the little Spiders would hear it rushing through the forest near by, and would feel their round brown house swinging like a cradle. It was fastened to a bush by the edge of the forest, but they could not know that, so they just wiggled and pushed and ate the food that they found in the house, and wondered what it all meant. They didn't even guess that a mother Spider had made the brown house and put the food in it for her Spider babies to eat when they came out of their eggs.

She had put the eggs in, too, but the little Spiders didn't remember the time when they lay curled up in the eggs. They didn't know what had been nor what was to be—they thought that to eat and wiggle and sleep was all of life. You see they had much to learn.

One morning the little Spiders found that the food was all gone, and they pushed and scrambled harder than ever, because they were hungry and wanted more. Exactly what happened nobody knew, but suddenly it grew light, and some of them fell out of the house. All the rest scrambled after, and there they stood, winking and blinking in the bright sunshine, and feeling a little bit dizzy, because they were on a shaky web made of silvery ropes.

Just then the web began to shake even more, and a beautiful great mother Spider ran out on it. She was dressed in black and yellow velvet, and her eight eyes glistened and gleamed in the sunlight. They had never dreamed of such a wonderful creature.

"Well, my children," she exclaimed, "I know you must be hungry, and I have breakfast all ready for you." So they began eating at once, and the mother Spider told them many things about the meadow and the forest, and said they must amuse themselves while she worked to get food for them. There was no father Spider to help her, and, as she said, "Growing children must have plenty of good plain food."

You can just fancy what a good time the baby Spiders had. There were a hundred and seventy of them, so they had no chance to grow lonely, even when their mother was away. They lived in this way for quite a while, and grew bigger and stronger every day. One morning the mother Spider said to her biggest daughter, "You are quite old enough to work now, and I will teach you to spin your web."

The little Spider soon learned to draw out the silvery ropes from the pocket in her body where they were made and kept, and very soon she had one fastened at both ends to branches of the bush. Then her mother made her walk out to the middle of her rope bridge, and spin and fasten two more, so that it looked like a shining cross. After that was done, the mother showed her something like a comb, which is part of a Spider's foot, and taught her how to measure, and put more ropes out from the middle of the cross, until it looked like the spokes of a wheel.

The little Spider got much discouraged, and said, "Let me finish it some other time; I am tired of working now."

The mother Spider answered, "No, I cannot have a lazy child."

The little one said, "I can't ever do it, I know I can't."

"Now," said the mother, "I shall have to give you a Spider scolding. You have acted as lazy as the Tree Frog says boys and girls sometimes do. He has been up near the farm-house, and says that he has seen there children who do not like to work. The meadow people could hardly believe such a thing at first. He says they were cross and unhappy children, and no wonder! Lazy people are never happy. You try to finish the web, and see if I am not right. You are not a baby now, and you must work and get your own food."

So the little Spider spun the circles of rope in the web, and made these ropes sticky, as all careful spiders do. She ate the loose ends and pieces that were left over, to save them for another time, and when it was done, it was so fine and perfect that her brothers and sisters crowded around, saying, "Oh! oh! oh! how beautiful!" and asked the mother to teach them. The little web-spinner was happier than she had ever been before, and the mother began to teach her other children. But it takes a long time to teach a hundred and seventy children.

THE BEETLE WHO DID NOT LIKE CATERPILLARS

ONE morning early in June, a fat and shining May Beetle lay on his back among the grasses, kicking his six legs in the air, and wriggling around while he tried to catch hold of a grass-blade by which to pull himself up. Now, Beetles do not like to lie on their backs in the sunshine, and this one was hot and tired from his long struggle. Beside that, he was very cross because he was late in getting his breakfast, so when he did at last get right side up, and saw a brown and black Caterpillar watching him, he grew very ill-mannered, and said some things of which he should have been ashamed.

"Oh, yes," he said, "you are quick enough to laugh when you think somebody else is in a fix. I often lie on my back and kick, just for fun." (Which was not true, but when Beetles are cross they are not always truthful.)

"Excuse me," said the Caterpillar, "I did not mean to hurt your feelings. If I smiled, it was because I remembered being in the same plight myself yesterday, and what a time I had smoothing my fur afterwards. Now, you won't have to smooth your fur, will you?" she asked pleasantly.

"No, I'm thankful to say I haven't any fur to smooth," snapped the Beetle. "I am not one of the crawling, furry kind. My family wear dark brown, glossy coats, and we always look trim and clean. When we want to hurry, we fly; and when tired of flying, we walk or run. We have two kinds of wings. We have a pair of dainty, soft ones, that carry us through the air, and then we have a pair of stiff ones to cover over the soft wings when we come down to the earth again. We are the finest family in the meadow."

"I have often heard of you," said the Caterpillar, "and am very glad to become acquainted."

"Well," answered the Beetle, "I am willing to speak to you, of course, but we can never be at all friendly. A May Beetle, indeed, in company with a Caterpillar! I choose my friends among the Moths, Butterflies, and Dragon-flies,—in fact, *I* move in the upper circles."

"Upper circles, indeed!" said a croaking voice beside him, which made the Beetle jump, "I have hopped over your head for two or three years, when you were nothing but a fat, white worm. *You'd* better not put on airs. The fine family of May Beetles were all worms once, and they had to live in the earth and eat roots, while the Caterpillars were in the sunshine over their heads, dining on tender green leaves and flower buds."

The May Beetle began to look very uncomfortable, and

squirmed as though he wanted to get away, but the Tree Frog, for it was the Tree Frog, went on: "As for your not liking Caterpillars, they don't stay Caterpillars. Your new acquaintance up there will come out with wings one of these days, and you will be glad enough to know him." And the Tree Frog hopped away.

The May Beetle scraped his head with his right front leg, and then said to the Caterpillar, who was nibbling away at the milkweed: "You know, I wasn't really in earnest about our not being friends. I shall be very glad to know you, and all your family."

"Thank you," answered the Caterpillar, "thank you very much, but I have been thinking it over myself, and I feel that I really could not be friendly with a May Beetle. Of course, I don't mind speaking to you once in a while, when I am eating, and getting ready to spin my cocoon. After that it will be different. You see, then I shall belong to one of the finest families in the meadow, the Milkweed Butterflies. *We* shall eat nothing but honey, and dress in soft orange and black velvet. *We* shall not blunder and bump around when we fly. *We* shall enjoy visiting with the Dragon-flies and Moths. I shall not forget you altogether, I dare say, but I shall feel it my duty to move in the upper circles, where I belong. Good-morning."

THE YOUNG ROBIN WHO
WAS AFRAID TO FLY.

DURING the days when the four beautiful green-blue eggs lay in the nest, Mrs. Robin stayed quite closely at home. She said it was a very good place, for she could keep her eggs warm and still see all that was happening. The rail-end on which they had built was on the meadow side of the fence, over the tallest grasses and the graceful stalks of golden-rod. Here the Garter Snake drew his shining body through the tangled green, and here the Tree Frog often came for a quiet nap.

Just outside the fence the milkweeds grew, with every broad, pale green leaf slanting upward in their spring style. Here the Milkweed Caterpillars fed, and here, too, when the great balls of tiny dull pink blossoms dangled from the stalks, the Milkweed Butterflies hung all day long. All the teams from the farm-house passed along the quiet, grass-grown road, and those which were going to the farm as well. When Mrs. Robin saw a team coming, she always settled herself more deeply into her nest, so that not one of her brick-red breast feathers showed. Then she sat very still, only turning her head enough to watch the team as it came near, passed, and went out of sight down the road.

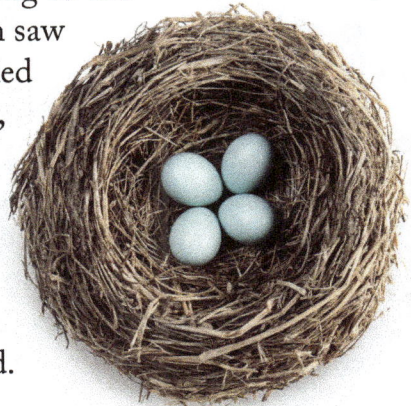

Sometimes she did not even have to turn her head, for if she happened to be facing the road, she could with one eye watch the team come near, and with the other watch it go away. No bird, you know, ever has to look at anything with both eyes at once.

After the young Robins had outgrown their shells and broken and thrown them off, they were naked and red and blind. They lay in a heap in the bottom of the nest, and became so tangled that nobody but a bird could tell which was which. If they heard their father or their mother flying toward them, they would stretch up their necks and open their mouths. Then each would have some food poked down his throat, and would lie still until another mouthful was brought to him.

When they got their eyes open and began to grow more down, they were good little Robins and did exactly as they were told. It was easy to be good then, for they were not strong enough to want to go elsewhere, and they had all they wanted to eat. At night their mother sat in the nest and covered them with her soft feathers. When it rained she also did this. She was a kind and very hard-working mother. Mr. Robin worked quite as hard as she, and was exceedingly proud of his family.

But when their feathers began to grow, and each young Robin's sharp quills pricked his brothers and sisters if they pushed against him, then it was not so easy to be good. Four growing children in one little round bed sometimes found themselves rather crowded. One night Mrs. Robin said to her husband: "I am all tired out. I work as long as daylight lasts getting food for those children, and I cannot be here enough to teach them anything."

"Then they must learn to work for themselves," said Mr. Robin decidedly. "They are surely old enough."

"Why, they are just babies!" exclaimed his wife. "They have hardly any tails yet."

"They don't need tails to eat with," said he, "and they may as well begin now. I will not have you get so tired for this one brood."

Mrs. Robin said nothing more. Indeed, there was nothing more to be said, for she knew perfectly well that her children would not eat with their tails if they had them. She loved her babies so that she almost disliked to see them grow up, yet she knew it was right for them to leave the nest. They were so large that they spread out over the edges of it already, and they must be taught to take care of themselves before it was time for her to rear her second brood.

The next morning all four children were made to hop out on to the rail. Their legs were not very strong and their toes sprawled weakly around. Sometimes they lurched and almost fell. Before leaving the nest they had felt big and very important; now they suddenly felt small and young and helpless. Once in a while one of them would hop feebly along the rail for a few steps. Then he would chirp in a frightened way, let his head settle down over his speckled breast, slide his eyelids over his eyes, and wait for more food to be brought to him.

Whenever a team went by, the oldest child shut his eyes. He thought they couldn't see him if he did that. The other children kept theirs open and watched to see what happened. Their father and mother had told them to watch, but the timid young Robin always shut his eyes in spite of that.

"We shall have trouble with him," said Mrs. Robin, "but he must be made to do as he is told, even if he is afraid." She shut her bill very tightly as she spoke, and Mr. Robin knew that he could safely trust the bringing-up of his timid son to her.

Mrs. Robin talked and talked to him, and still he shut his eyes every time that he was frightened. "I can't keep them open," he would say, "because when I am frightened I am always afraid, and I can't be brave when I am afraid."

"That is just when you must be brave," said his mother. "There is no use in being brave when there is nothing to fear, and it is a great deal braver to be brave when you are frightened than to be brave when you are not." You can see that she was a very wise Robin and a good mother. It would have been dreadful for her to let him grow up a coward.

At last the time came when the young birds were to fly to the ground and hop across the road. Both their father and their mother were there to show them how. "You must

let go of the rail," they said. "You will never fly in the world unless you let go of the rail."

Three of the children fluttered and lurched and flew down. The timid young Robin would not try it. His father ordered and his mother coaxed, yet he only clung more closely to his rail and said, "I can't! I'm afraid!"

At last his mother said: "Very well. You shall stay there as long as you wish, but we cannot stay with you."

Then she chirped to her husband, and they and the three brave children went across the road, talking as they went. "Careful!" she would say. "Now another hop! That was fine! Now another!" And the father fluttered around and said: "Good! Good! You'll be grown-up before you know it." When they were across, the parents hunted food and fed their three brave children, tucking the mouthfuls far into their wide-open bills.

The timid little Robin on the fence felt very, very lonely. He was hungry, too. Whenever he saw his mother pick up a mouthful of food, he chirped loudly: "Me! Me! Me!" for he wanted her to bring it to him. She paid no attention to him for a long time. Then she called: "Do you think you can fly? Do you think you can fly? Do you think?"

The timid little Robin hopped a few steps and chirped but never lifted a wing. Then his mother gave each of the other children a big mouthful.

The Robin on the fence huddled down into a miserable little bunch, and thought: "They don't care whether I ever have anything to eat. No, they don't!" Then he heard a rush of wings, and his mother stood before him with a bunch in her bill for him. He hopped toward her and she ran away.

Then he sat down and cried. She hopped back and looked lovingly at him, but couldn't speak because her bill was so full. Across the road the Robin father stayed with his brave children and called out, "Earn it, my son, earn it!"

The young Robin stretched out his neck and opened his bill—but his mother flew to the ground. He was so hungry—so very, very hungry,—that for a minute he quite forgot to be afraid, and he leaned toward her and toppled over. He fluttered his wings without thinking, and the first he knew he had flown to the ground. He was hardly there before his mother was feeding him and his father was singing: "Do you know what you did? Do you know what you did? Do you know?"

Before his tail was grown the timid Robin had become as brave as any of the children, for, you know, after you begin to be brave you always want to go on. But the Garter Snake says that Mrs. Robin is the bravest of the family.

THE CRICKET'S SCHOOL

IN one corner of the meadow lived a fat old Cricket, who thought a great deal of himself. He had such a big, shining body, and a way of chirping so very loudly, that nobody could ever forget where he lived. He was a very good sort of Cricket, too, ready to say the most pleasant things to everybody, yet, sad to relate, he had a dreadful habit of boasting. He had not always lived in the meadow, and he liked to tell of the wonderful things he had seen and done when he was younger and lived up near the white farm-house.

When he told these stories of what he had done, the big Crickets around him would not say much, but just sit and look at each other. The little Crickets, however, loved to hear him talk, and would often come to the door of his house (which was a hole in the ground), to beg him to tell them more.

One evening he said he would teach them a few things

that all little Crickets should know. He had them stand in a row, and then began: "With what part of your body do you eat?"

"With our mouths," all the little Crickets shouted.

"With what part of your body do you run and leap?"

"Our legs," they cried.

"Do you do anything else with your legs?"

"We clean ourselves with them," said one.

"We use them and our mouths to make our houses in the ground," said another.

"Oh yes, and we hear with our two front legs," cried one bright little fellow.

"That is right," answered the fat old Cricket. "Some creatures hear with things called ears, that grow on the sides of their heads, but for my part, I think it much nicer to hear with one's legs, as we do."

"Why, how funny it must be not to hear with one's legs, as we do," cried all the little Crickets together.

"There are a great many queer things to be seen in the great world," said their teacher. "I have seen some terribly big creatures with only two legs and no wings whatever."

"How dreadful!" all the little Crickets cried. "We wouldn't think they could move about at all."

"It must be very hard to do so," said their teacher; "I was

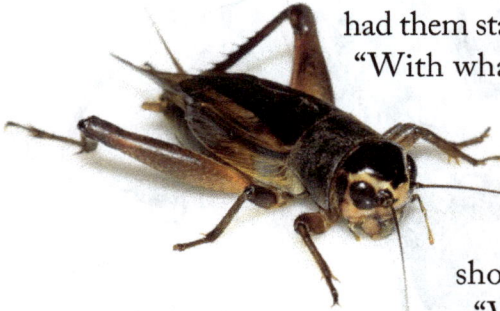

very sorry for them," and he spread out his own wings and stretched his six legs to show how he enjoyed them.

"But how can they sing if they have no wings?" asked the bright little Cricket.

"They sing through their mouths, in much the same way that the birds have to. I am sure it must be much easier to sing by rubbing one's wings together, as we do," said the fat old teacher. "I could tell you many queer things about these two-legged creatures, and the houses in which they live, and perhaps some day I will. There are other large four-legged creatures around their homes that are very terrible, but, my children, I was never afraid of any of them. I am one of the truly brave people who are never frightened, no matter how terrible the sight. I hope, children, that you will always be brave, like me. If anything should scare you, do not jump or run away. Stay right where you are, and—"

But the little Crickets never heard the rest of what their teacher began to say, for at that minute Brown Bess, the Cow, came through a broken fence toward the spot where the Crickets were. The teacher gave one shrill "chirp," and scrambled down his hole. The little Crickets fairly tumbled over each other in their hurry to get away, and the fat old Cricket, who had been out in the great world, never again talked to them about being brave.

THE CONTENTED EARTHWORMS

AFTER a long and soaking rain, the Earthworms came out of their burrows, or rather, they came part way out, for each Earthworm put out half of his body, and, as there were many of them and they lived near to each other, they could easily visit without leaving their own homes. Two of these long, slimy people were talking, when a Potato Bug strolled by. "You poor things," said he, "what a wretched life you must lead. Spending one's days in the dark earth must be very dreary."

"Dreary!" exclaimed one of the Earthworms, "it is delightful. The earth is a snug and soft home. It is warm in cold weather and cool in warm weather. There are no winds to trouble us, and no sun to scorch us."

"But," said the Potato Bug, "it must be very dull. Now, out in the grass, one finds beautiful flowers, and so many families of friends."

"And down here," answered the

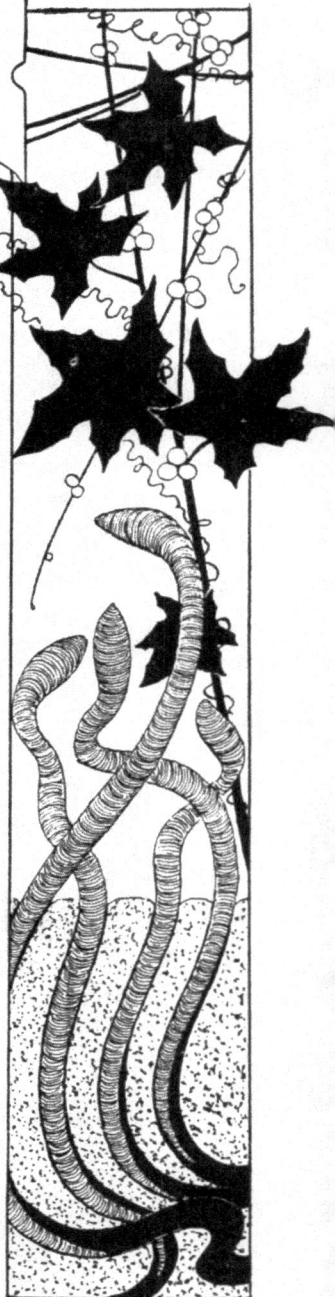

44

Worm, "we have the roots. Some are brown and woody, like those of the trees, and some are white and slender and soft. They creep and twine, until it is like passing through a forest to go among them. And then, there are the seeds. Such busy times as there are in the ground in spring-time! Each tiny seed awakens and begins to grow. Its roots must strike downward, and its stalk upward toward the light. Sometimes the seeds are buried in the earth with the root end up, and then they have a great time getting twisted around and ready to grow."

"Still, after the plants are all growing and have their heads in the air, you must miss them."

"We have the roots always," said the Worm. "And then, when the summer is over, the plants have done their work, helping to make the world beautiful and raise their seed babies, and they wither and droop to the earth again, and little by little the sun and the frost and the rain help them to melt back into the earth. The earth is the beginning and the end of plants."

"Do you ever meet the meadow people in it?" asked the Potato Bug.

"Many of them live here as babies," said the Worm. "The May Beetles, the Grasshoppers, the great Humming-bird Moths, and many others spend their babyhood here, all wrapped in eggs or cocoons. Then, when they are strong enough, and their legs and wings are grown, they push their way out and begin their work. It is

their getting-ready time, down
here in the dark. And then,
there are the stones, and
they are so old and queer.
I am often glad that I am
not a stone, for to have to lie
still must be hard to bear. Yet I have heard that they did
not always lie so, and that some of the very pebbles around
us tossed and rolled and ground for years in the bed of a
river, and that some of them were rubbed and broken off of
great rocks. Perhaps they are glad now to just lie and rest."

"Truly," said the Potato Bug, "you have a pleasant home,
but give me the sunshine and fresh air, my six legs, and my
striped wings, and you are welcome to it all."

"You are welcome to them all," answered the Worms.
"We are contented with smooth and shining bodies, with
which we can bore and wriggle our way through the soft,
brown earth. We like our task of keeping the earth right
for the plants, and we will work and rest happily here."

The Potato Bug went his way, and said to his brothers, "What do you think? I have been talking with
Earthworms who would not be Potato Bugs if they
could." And they all shook their heads in wonder, for
they thought that to be Potato Bugs
was the grandest and happiest
thing in the world.

THE MEASURING WORM'S JOKE

ONE day there crawled over the meadow fence a jolly young Measuring Worm. He came from a bush by the roadside, and although he was still a young Worm he had kept his eyes open and had a very good idea how things go in this world. "Now," thought he, as he rested on the top rail of the fence, "I shall meet some new friends. I do hope they will be pleasant. I will look about me and see if anyone is in sight." So he raised his head high in the air and, sure enough, there were seven Caterpillars of different kinds on a tall clump of weeds near by.

The Measuring Worm hurried over to where they were, and making his

best bow said: "I have just come from the roadside and think I shall live in the meadow. May I feed with you?"

The Caterpillars were all glad to have him, and he joined their party. He asked many questions about the meadow, and the people who lived there, and the best place to find food. The Caterpillars said, "Oh, the meadow is a good place, and the people are nice enough, but they are not at all fashionable—not at all."

"Why," said the Measuring Worm, "if you have nice people and a pleasant place in which to live, I don't see what more you need."

"That is all very well," said a black and yellow Caterpillar, "but what we want is fashionable society. The meadow people always do things in the same way, and one gets so tired of that. Now can you not tell us something different, something that Worms do in the great world from which you come?"

Just at this minute the Measuring Worm had a funny idea, and he wondered if the Caterpillars would be foolish enough to copy him. He thought it would be a good joke if they did, so he said very soberly, "I notice that when you walk you keep your body quite close to the

ground. I have seen many Worms do the same thing, and it is all right if they wish to, but none of my family ever do so. Did you notice how I walk?"

"Yes, yes," cried the Caterpillars, "show us again."

So the Measuring Worm walked back and forth for them, arching his body as high as he could, and stopping every little while to raise his head and look haughtily around.

"What grace!" exclaimed the Caterpillars. "What grace, and what style!" and one black and brown one tried to walk in the same way.

The Measuring Worm wanted to laugh to see how awkward the black and brown Caterpillar was, but he did not even smile, and soon every one of the Caterpillars was trying the same thing, and saying "Look at me. Don't I do well?" or, "How was that?"

You can just imagine how those seven Caterpillars looked when trying to walk like the Measuring Worm. Every few minutes one of them would tumble over, and they all got warm and tired. At last they thought they had learned it very well, and took a long rest, in which they planned to take a long walk and show the other meadow people the fashion they had received from the outside world.

"We will walk in a line," they said, "as far as we can, and

let them all see us. Ah, it will be a great day for the meadow when we begin to set the fashions!"

The mischievous young Measuring Worm said not a word, and off they started. The big black and yellow Caterpillar went first, the black and brown one next, and so on down to the smallest one at the end of the line, all arching their bodies as high as they could. All the meadow people stared at them, calling each other to come and look, and whenever the Caterpillars reached a place where there were many watching them, they would all raise their heads and look around exactly as the Measuring Worm had done. When they got back to their clump of bushes, they had the most dreadful backaches, but they said to each other, "Well, we have been fashionable for once."

And, at the same time, out in the grass, the meadow people were saying, "Did you ever see anything so ridiculous in your life?" All of which goes to show how very silly people sometimes are when they think too much of being fashionable.

A PUZZLED CICADA

SEVENTEEN years is a long, long time to be getting ready to fly; yet that is what the Seventeen-year Locusts, or Cicadas, have to expect. First, they lie for a long time in eggs, down in the earth. Then, when they awaken, and crawl out of their shells, they must grow strong enough to dig before they can make their way out to where the beautiful green grass is growing and waving in the wind.

The Cicada who got so very much puzzled had not been long out of his home in the warm, brown earth. He was the only Cicada anywhere around, and it was very lonely for him. However, he did not mind

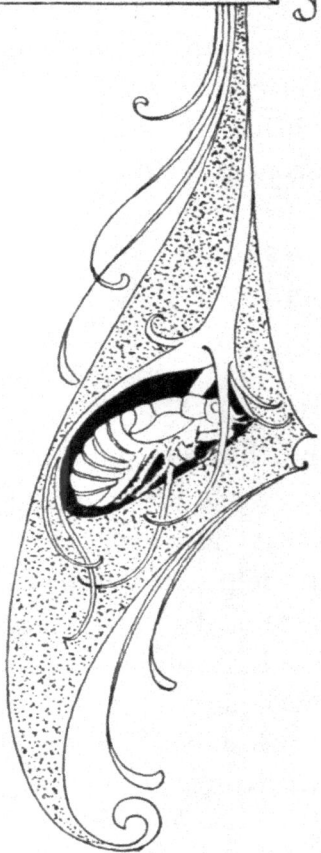

that so much when he was eating, or singing, or resting in the sunshine, and as he was either eating, or singing, or resting in the sunshine most of the time, he got along fairly well.

Because he was young and healthy he grew fast. He grew so very fast that after a while he began to feel heavy and stiff, and more like sitting still than like crawling around. Beside all this, his skin got tight, and you can imagine how uncomfortable it must be to have one's skin too tight. He was sitting on the branch of a bush one day, thinking about the wonderful great world, when—pop!—his skin had cracked open right down the middle of his back! The poor Cicada was badly frightened at first, but then it seemed so good and roomy that he took a deep breath, and—pop!—the crack was longer still!

The Cicada found that he had another whole skin under the outside one which had cracked, so he thought, "How much cooler and more comfortable I shall be if I crawl out of this broken covering," and out he crawled.

It wasn't very easy work, because he didn't have anybody to help him. He had to hook the claws of his outer skin into the bark of the branch, hook them in so hard that they couldn't pull out, and then he began to wriggle out of the back of his own skin. It was exceedingly hard work, and the hardest of all was the pulling his legs out of their cases. He was so tired when he got free that he could hardly think, and his new skin was so soft and tender that he felt limp and queer. He found that he had wings of a pretty green, the same color as his legs. He knew these wings must have been growing under his old skin, and he stretched them slowly out to see how big they were. This was in the morning, and after he had stretched his wings he went to sleep for a long time.

When he awakened, the sun was in the western sky, and he tried to think who he was. He looked at himself, and instead of being green he was a dull brown and black. Then he saw his old skin clinging to the branch and staring him in the face. It was just the same shape as when he was in it, and he thought for a minute that he was dreaming. He rubbed his head hard with his front legs to make sure he was awake, and then he began to wonder which one he was. Sometimes he thought that the old skin which clung to the bush was the Cicada that had lain so long in the ground, and sometimes he thought that the soft, fat, new-looking one was the Cicada. Or were both of them the Cicada? If he were only one of the two, what would he do with the other?

While he was wondering about this in a sleepy way, an old Cicada from across the river flew down beside him. He thought he would ask her, so he waved his feelers as politely as he knew how, and said, "Excuse me, Madam Cicada, for I am much puzzled. It took me seventeen years to grow into

a strong, crawling Cicada, and then in one day I separated. The thinking, moving part of me is here, but the outside shell of me is there on that branch. Now, which part is the real Cicada?"

"Why, that is easy enough," said the Madam Cicada; "You are *you*, of course. The part that you cast off and left clinging to the branch was very useful once. It kept you warm on cold days and cool on warm days, and you needed it while you were only a crawling creature. But when your wings were ready to carry you off to a higher and happier life, then the skin that had been a help was in your way, and you did right to wriggle out of it. It is no longer useful to you. Leave it where it is and fly off to enjoy your new life. You will never have trouble if you remember that the thinking part is the real *you*."

And then Madam Cicada and her new friend flew away to her home over the river, and he saw many strange sights before he returned to the meadow.

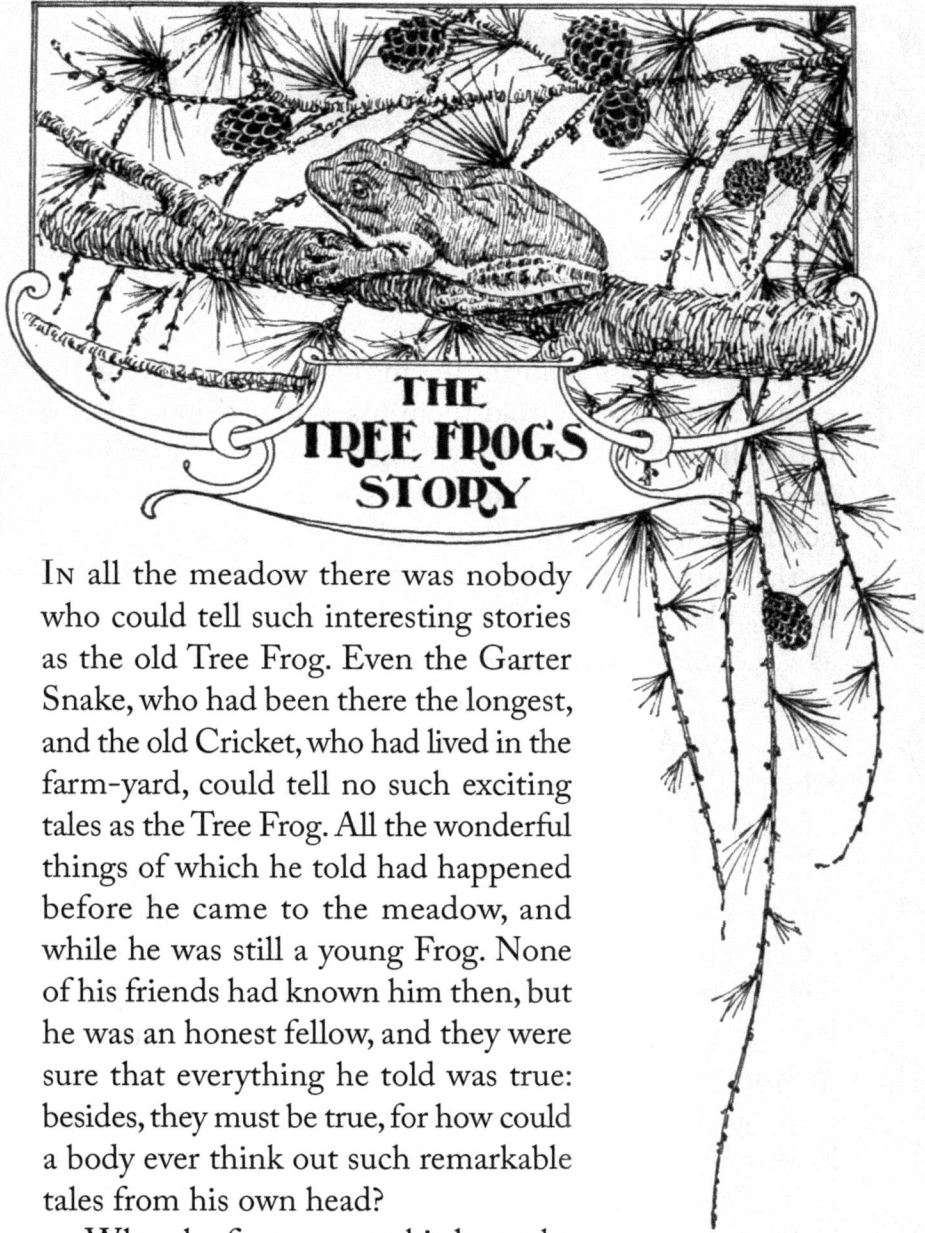

THE
TREE FROG'S
STORY

In all the meadow there was nobody who could tell such interesting stories as the old Tree Frog. Even the Garter Snake, who had been there the longest, and the old Cricket, who had lived in the farm-yard, could tell no such exciting tales as the Tree Frog. All the wonderful things of which he told had happened before he came to the meadow, and while he was still a young Frog. None of his friends had known him then, but he was an honest fellow, and they were sure that everything he told was true: besides, they must be true, for how could a body ever think out such remarkable tales from his own head?

When he first came to his home by

the elm tree he was very thin, and looked as though he had been sick. The Katydids who stayed near said that he croaked in his sleep, and that, you know, is not what well and happy Frogs should do.

One day when many of the meadow people were gathered around him, he told them his story. "When I was a little fellow," he said, "I was strong and well, and could leap farther than any other Frog of my size. I was hatched in the pond beyond the farm-house, and ate my way from the egg to the water outside like any other Frog. Perhaps I ought to say, 'like any other Tadpole,' for, of course, I began life as a Tadpole. I played and ate with my brothers and sisters, and little dreamed what trouble was in store for me when I grew up. We were all in a hurry to be Frogs, and often talked of what we would do and how far we would travel when we were grown.

"Oh, how happy we were then! I remember the day when my hind legs began to grow, and how the other Tadpoles crowded around me in the water and swam close to me to feel the two little bunches that were to be legs. My fore legs did not grow until later, and these bunches came just in front of my tail."

"Your tail!" cried a puzzled young Cricket; "why, you haven't any tail!"

"I did have when I was a Tadpole," said the Tree Frog. "I had a beautiful, wiggly little tail with which to swim

through the waters of the pond; but as my legs grew larger
and stronger, my tail grew littler and weaker, until there
wasn't any tail left. By the time my tail was gone
I had four good legs, and could breathe
through both my nose and my skin.
The knobs on the ends of my toes
were sticky, so that I could
climb a tree, and then I was
ready to start on my travels.
Some of the other Frogs started
with me, but they stopped along the
way, and at last I was alone.

"I was a bold young fellow, and when I saw a great white
thing among the trees up yonder, I made up my mind to see
what it was. There was a great red thing in the yard beside
it, but I liked the white one better. I hopped along as fast as
I could, for I did not then know enough to be afraid. I got
close up to them both, and saw strange, big creatures going
in and out of the red thing—the barn, as I afterward found
it was called. The largest creatures had four legs, and some of
them had horns. The smaller creatures had only two legs on
which to walk, and two other limbs of some sort with which
they lifted and carried things. The queerest thing about it
was, that the smaller creatures seemed to make the larger
ones do whatever they wanted them to. They even made
some of them help do their work. You may not believe me,
but what I tell you is true. I saw two of the larger ones tied
to a great load of dried grass and pulling it into the barn.

"As you may guess, I stayed there a long time, watching
these strange creatures work. Then I went over toward the

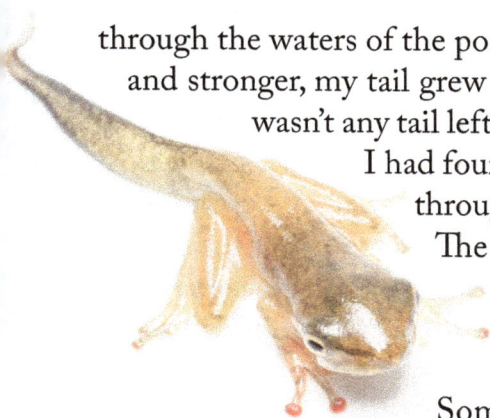

white thing, and that, I found out, was the farm-house. Here were more of the two-legged creatures, but they were dressed differently from those in the barn. There were some bright-colored flowers near the house, and I crawled in among them. There I rested until sunset, and then began my evening song. While I was singing, one of the people from the house came out and found me. She picked me up and carried me inside. Oh, how frightened I was! My heart thumped as though it would burst, and I tried my best to get away from her. She didn't hurt me at all, but she would not let me go.

"She put me in a very queer prison. At first, when she put me down on a stone in some water, I did not know that I was in prison. I tried to hop away, and—bump! went my head against something. Yet when I drew back, I could see no wall there. I tried it again and again, and every time I hurt my head. I tell you the truth, my friends, those walls were made of something which one could see through."

"Wonderful!" exclaimed all the meadow people; "wonderful, indeed!"

"And at the top," continued the Tree Frog, "was something white over the doorway into my prison. In the bottom were water and a stone, and from the bottom to the top was a ladder. There I had to live for most of the summer. I had enough to eat; but anybody who has been free cannot be happy shut in. I watched my chance, and three times I got out when the little door was not quite closed. Twice I was caught and put back. In the pleasant weather, of course, I went to the top of the ladder, and when it was going to rain I would go down again. Every time that I went up or down, those dreadful creatures would put their faces up close to my prison, and I could hear a roaring sound which meant they were talking and laughing.

"The last time I got out, I hid near the door of the house, and although they hunted and hunted for me, they didn't find me. After they stopped hunting, the wind blew the door open, and I hopped out."

"You don't say!" exclaimed a Grasshopper.

"Yes, I hopped out and scrambled away through the grass as fast as ever I could. You people who have never been in prison cannot think how happy I was. It seemed to me that just stretching my legs was enough to make me wild with joy. Well, I came right here, and you were all kind to me, but for a long time I could not sleep without dreaming that I was back in prison, and I would croak in my sleep at the thought of it."

"I heard you," cried the Katydid, "and I wondered what was the matter."

"Matter enough," said the Tree Frog. "It makes my skin dry to think of it now. And, friends, the best way I can ever repay your kindness to me, is to tell you to never, never, never, never go near the farm-house."

And they all answered, "We never will."

THE DAY
WHEN
THE GRASS
WAS CUT.

THERE came a day when all the meadow people rushed back and forth, waving their feelers and talking hurriedly to each other. The fat old Cricket was nowhere to be seen. He said that one of his legs was lame and he thought it best to stay quietly in his hole. The young Crickets thought he was afraid. Perhaps he was, but he said that he was lame.

All the insects who had holes crawled into them carrying food. Everybody was anxious and fussy, and some people were even cross. It was all because the farmer and his men had come into the meadow to cut the grass. They began to work on the side nearest the road, but every step which the Horses took brought the mower nearer to the people who lived in the middle of the meadow or down toward the river.

"I have seen this done before," said the Garter Snake. "I got away from the big mower, and hid in the grass by the trees, or by the stumps where the mower couldn't come. Then the men came and cut that grass with their scythes, and I had to wriggle away over the short, sharp grass-stubble to my hole. When they get near me this time, I shall go into my hole and stay there."

"They are not so bad after all," said the Tree Frog. "I like them better out-of-doors than I did in the house. They saw me out here once and didn't try to catch me."

A Meadow Mouse came hurrying along. "I must get home to my babies," she said. "They will be frightened if I am not there."

"Much good you can do when you are there!" growled a voice down under her feet. She was standing over the hole where the fat old Cricket was with his lame leg.

The mother Meadow Mouse looked rather angry for a minute, and then she answered: "I'm not so very large and strong, but I can squeak and let the Horses know where the nest is. Then they won't step on it. Last year I had ten or twelve babies there, and one of the men picked them up and looked at them and then put them back. I was so frightened that my fur stood on end and I shook like June grass in the wind."

"Humph! Too scared to run away," said the voice under her feet.

"Mothers don't run away and leave their children in danger," answered the Meadow Mouse. "I think it is a great deal braver to be brave when you are afraid than it is to be brave when you're not afraid." She whisked her long tail and scampered off through the grass. She did not go the nearest way to her nest because she thought the Garter Snake might be watching. She didn't wish him to know where she lived. She knew he was fond of young Mice, and didn't want him to come to see her babies while she was away. She said he was not a good friend for young children.

"We don't mind it at all," said the

Mosquitoes from the lower part of the meadow. "We are unusually hungry today anyway, and we shall enjoy having the men come."

"Nothing to make such a fuss over," said a Milkweed Butterfly. "Just crawl into your holes or fly away."

"Sometimes they step on the holes and close them," said an Ant. "What would you do if you were in a hole and it stopped being a hole and was just earth?"

"Crawl out, I suppose," answered the Milkweed Butterfly with a careless flutter.

"Yes," said the Ant, "but I don't see what there would be to crawl out through."

The Milkweed Butterfly was already gone. Butterflies never worry about anything very long, you know.

"Has anybody seen the Measuring Worm?" asked the Katydid. "Where is he?"

"Oh, I'm up a tree," answered a pleasant voice above their heads, "but I sha'n't be up a tree very long. I shall come down when the grass is cut."

"Oh, dear, dear, dear!" cried the Ants, hurrying around. "We can't think what we want to do. We don't know what we ought to do. We can't think and we don't know, and we don't think that we ought to!"

"Click!" said a Grasshopper, springing into the air. "We must hurry, hurry, hurry!" He jumped from a stalk of pepper-grass to a plantain. "We *must* hurry," he said, and he jumped from the plantain back to the pepper-grass.

Up in the tree where the Measuring Worm was, some Katydids were sitting on a branch and singing shrilly: "Did you ever? Did you ever? Ever? Ever? Ever? Did you ever?" And this shows how much excited they were, for they usually sang only at night.

Then the mower came sweeping down the field, drawn by the Blind Horse and the Dappled Gray, and guided by the farmer himself. The dust rose in clouds as they passed, the Grasshoppers gave mighty springs which took them out of the way, and all the singing and shrilling stopped until the mower had passed. The nodding grasses swayed and fell as the sharp knives slid over the ground. "We are going to be hay," they said, "and live in the big barn."

"Now we shall grow some more tender green blades," said the grass roots.

"Fine weather for haying," snorted the Dappled Gray. "We'll cut all the grass in this field before noon."

"Good feeling ground to walk on," said the Blind Horse, tossing his head until the harness jingled.

Then the Horses and the farmer and the mower passed far away, and the meadow people came together again.

"Well," said the Tree Frog. "That's over for a while."

The Ants and the Grasshoppers came back to their old

places. "We did just the right thing," they cried joyfully. "We got out of the way."

The Measuring Worm and the Katydids came down from their tree as the Milkweed Butterfly fluttered past. "The men left the grass standing around the Meadow Mouse's nest," said the Milkweed Butterfly, "and the Cows up by the barn are telling how glad they will be to have the hay when the cold weather comes."

"Grass must grow and hay be cut," said the wise old Tree Frog, "and when the time comes we always know what to do. Puk-rup! Puk-r-r-rup!"

"I think," said the fat old Cricket, as he crawled out of his hole, "that my lame leg is well enough to use. There is nothing like rest for a lame leg."

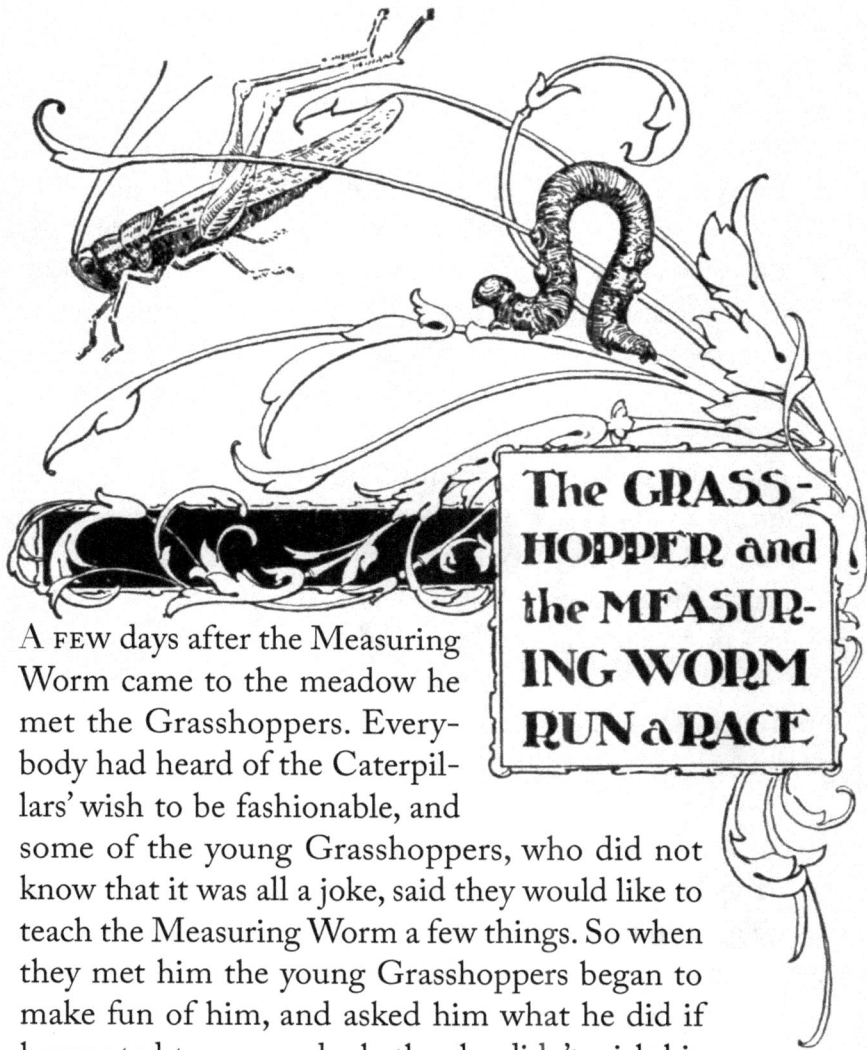

The GRASS-HOPPER and the MEASUR-ING WORM RUN a RACE

A FEW days after the Measuring Worm came to the meadow he met the Grasshoppers. Everybody had heard of the Caterpillars' wish to be fashionable, and some of the young Grasshoppers, who did not know that it was all a joke, said they would like to teach the Measuring Worm a few things. So when they met him the young Grasshoppers began to make fun of him, and asked him what he did if he wanted to run, and whether he didn't wish his head grew on the middle of his back so that he could see better when walking.

The Measuring Worm was good-natured, and only said that he found his head useful where it was. Soon one fine-looking Grasshopper asked him to race. "That will show," said the Grasshopper, "which is the better traveller."

The Measuring Worm said: "Certainly, I will race with you to-morrow, and we will ask all our friends to look on." Then he began talking about something else. He was a wise young fellow, as well as a jolly one, and he knew the Grasshoppers felt sure that he would be beaten. "If I cannot win the race by swift running," thought he, "I must try to win it by good planning." So he got the Grasshoppers to go with him to a place where the sweet young grass grew, and they all fed together.

The Measuring Worm nibbled only a little here and there, but he talked a great deal about the sweetness of the grass, and how they would not get any more for a long time because the hot weather would spoil it. And the Grasshoppers said to each other: "He is right, and we must eat all we can while we have it." So they ate, and ate, and ate, and ate, until sunset, and in the morning they awakened and began eating again. When the time for the race came, they were all heavy and stupid from so much eating,—which was exactly what the Measuring Worm wanted.

The Tree Frog, the fat, old Cricket, and a Caterpillar were chosen to be the judges, and the race was to be a long one,—from the edge of the woods to the fence. When the meadow people were all gathered around to see the race, the Cricket gave a shrill chirp, which meant "Go!" and off they started. That is to say, the Measuring Worm started. The Grasshopper felt so sure he could beat that he wanted to give the Measuring Worm a little the start, because then, you see, he could say he had won without half trying.

The Measuring Worm started off at a good, steady rate, and when he had gone a few feet the Grasshopper gave a couple of great leaps, which landed him far ahead of the Worm. Then he stopped to nibble a blade of grass and visit with some Katydids who were looking on. By and by he took a few more leaps and passed the Measuring Worm again. This time he began to show off by jumping up straight into the air, and when he came down he would call out to those who stood near to see how strong he was and how easy it would be for him to win the race. And everybody said, "How strong he is, to be sure!" "What wonderful legs he has!" and "He could beat the Measuring Worm with his eyes shut!" which made the Grasshopper so exceedingly vain that he stopped more and more often to show his strength and daring.

That was the way it went, until they were only a short distance from the end of the race course. The Grasshopper was more and more pleased to think how easily he was winning, and stopped for a last time to nibble grass and make fun of the Worm. He gave a great leap into the air, and when he came down there was the Worm on the fence! All the meadow people croaked, and shrilled, and chirped to see the way in which the race ended, and the Grasshopper was very much vexed. "You shouldn't call him the winner," he said; "I can travel ten times as fast as he, if I try."

"Yes," answered the judges, "we all know that, yet the winning of the race is not decided by what you might do, but by what you did do." And the meadow people all cried: "Long live the Measuring Worm! Long live the Measuring Worm!"

MR GREEN FROG AND HIS VISITORS

ONE day a young Frog who lived down by the river, came hopping up through the meadow. He was a fine-looking fellow, all brown and green, with a white vest, and he came to see the sights. The oldest Frog on the river bank had told him that he ought to travel and learn to know the world, so he had started at once.

Young Mr. Green Frog had very big eyes, and they stuck out from his head more than ever when he saw all the strange sights and heard all the strange sounds of the meadow. Yet he made one great mistake, just as bigger and

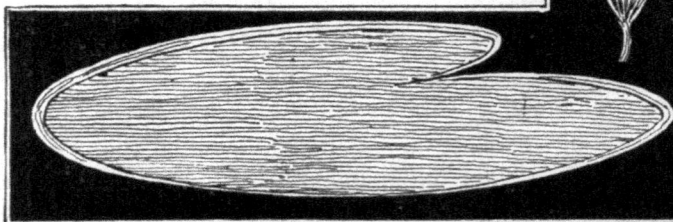

better people sometimes do when they go on a journey; he didn't try to learn from the things he saw, but only to show off to the meadow people how much he already knew, and he boasted a great deal of the fine way in which he lived when at home.

Mr. Green Frog told those whom he met that the meadow was dreadfully dry, and that he really could not see how they lived there. He said they ought to see the lovely soft mud that there was in the marsh, and that there the people could sit all day with their feet in water in among the rushes where the sunshine never came. "And then," he said, "to eat grass as the Grasshoppers did! If they would go home with him, he would show them how to live."

The older Grasshoppers and Crickets and Locusts only looked at each other and opened their funny mouths in a smile, but the young ones thought Mr. Green Frog must be right, and they wanted to go back with him. The old Hoppers told them that they wouldn't like it down there, and that they would be sorry that they had gone; still the young ones teased and teased and teased and teased until everybody said: "Well, let them go, and then perhaps they will be contented when they return."

At last they all set off together,— Mr. Green Frog and the young meadow people. Mr. Green Frog

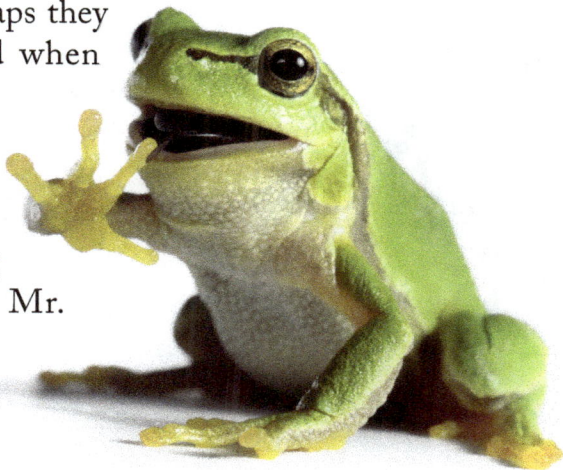

took little jumps all the way and bragged and bragged. The Grasshoppers went in long leaps, the Crickets scampered most of the way, and the Locusts fluttered. It was a very gay little party, and they kept saying to each other, "What a fine time we shall have!"

When they got to the marsh, Mr. Green Frog went in first with a soft "plunk" in the mud. The rest all followed and tried to make believe that they liked it, but they didn't—they didn't at all. The Grasshoppers kept bumping against the tough, hard rushes when they jumped, and then that would tumble them over on their backs in the mud, and there they would lie, kicking their legs in the air, until some friendly Cricket pushed them over on their feet again. The Locusts couldn't fly at all there, and the Crickets got their shiny black coats all grimy and horrid.

They all got cold and wet and tired—yes, and hungry too, for there were no tender green things growing in among the rushes. Still they pretended to have a good time, even while they were thinking how they would like to be in their dear old home.

After the sun went down in the west it grew

colder still, and all the Frogs in the marsh began to croak to the moon, croaking so loudly that the tired little travellers could not sleep at all. When the Frogs stopped croaking and went to sleep in the mud, one tired Cricket said: "If you like this, *stay*. I am going home as fast as my six little legs will carry me." And all the rest of the travellers said: "So am I," "So am I," "So am I."

Mr. Green Frog was sleeping soundly, and they crept away as quietly as they could out into the silvery moonlight and up the bank towards home. Such a tired little party as they were, and so hungry that they had to stop and eat every little while. The dew was on the grass and they could not get warm.

The sun was just rising behind the eastern forest when they got home. They did not want to tell about their trip at all, but just ate a lot of pepper-grass to make them warm, and then rolled themselves in between the woolly mullein leaves to rest all day long. And that was the last time any of them ever went away with a stranger.

THE DIGNIFIED
WALKING-STICKS.

THREE Walking-Sticks from the forest had come to live in the big maple tree near the middle of the meadow. Nobody knew exactly why they had left the forest, where all their sisters and cousins and aunts lived. Perhaps they were not happy with their relatives. But then, if one is a Walking-Stick, you know, one does not care so very much about one's family.

These Walking-Sticks had grown up the best way they could, with no father or mother to care for them. They had never been taught to do anything useful, or to think much about other people. When they were hungry they ate some leaves, and never thought what they should eat the next time that they happened to be hungry. When they were tired they went to sleep, and when they had slept enough they awakened. They had nothing to do but to eat and sleep, and they did not often take the trouble to think. They felt that they were a little better than those meadow people who rushed and scrambled and worked from morning until night, and they showed very plainly how they felt. They said it was not genteel to hurry, no matter what happened.

One day the Tree Frog was under the tree when the large Brown Walking-Stick decided to lay some eggs. He saw her dropping them carelessly around on the ground, and asked, "Do you never fix a place for your eggs?"

"A place?" said the Brown Walking-Stick, waving her long and slender feelers to and fro. "A place? Oh, no! I think they will hatch where they are. It is too much trouble to find a place."

"Puk-r-r-rup!" said the Tree Frog. "Some mothers do not think it too much trouble to be careful where they lay eggs."

"That may be," said the Brown Walking-Stick, "but they do not belong to our family." She spoke as if those who did not belong to her family might be good but could never be genteel. She had once told her brother, the Five-Legged Walking-Stick, that she would not want to live if she could not be genteel. She thought the meadow people very common.

The Five-Legged Walking-Stick looked much like his sister. He had the same long, slender body, the same long feelers, and the same sort of long, slender legs. If you had passed them in a hay-field, you would surely have thought each a stem of hay, unless you happened to see them move.

The other Walking-Stick, their friend, was younger and green. You would have thought her a blade of grass.

It is true that the brother had the same kind of legs as his sister, but he did not have the same number. When he was young and green he had six, then came a dreadful day when a hungry Nuthatch saw him, flew down, caught him, and carried him up a tree. He knew just what to expect, so when the Nuthatch set him down on the bark to look at him, he unhooked his feet from the bark and tumbled to the ground. The Nuthatch tried to catch him and broke off one of his legs, but she never found him again, although she looked and looked and looked and looked. That was because he crawled into a clump of ferns and kept very still.

His sister came and looked at him and said, "Now if you were only a Spider it would not be long before you would have six legs again."

Her brother waved first one feeler and then the other, and said: "Do you think I would be a Spider for the sake of growing legs? I would rather be a Walking-Stick without any legs than to be a Spider with a hundred." Of course, you know, Spiders never do have a hundred, and a Walking-Stick wouldn't be walking without any, but that was just his way of speaking, and it showed what kind of insect he was. His relatives all waved their feelers, one at a time, and said, "Ah, he has the true Walking-Stick spirit!" Then they paid no more attention to him, and after a while he and his sister and their green little friend left the forest for the meadow.

On the day when the grass was cut, they had sat quietly in their trees and looked genteel. Their feelers were held quite close together, and they did not move their feet at all, only swayed their bodies gracefully from side to side. Now they were on the ground, hunting through the flat piles of cut grass for some fresh and juicy bits to eat. The Tree Frog was also out, sitting in a cool, damp corner of the grass rows. The young Grasshoppers were kicking up their feet, the Ants were scrambling around as busy as ever, and life went on quite as though neither men nor Horses had ever entered the meadow.

"See!" cried a Spider who was busily looking after her web, "there comes a Horse drawing something, and the farmer sitting on it and driving."

When the Horse was well into the meadow, the farmer moved a bar, and the queer-looking machine began to kick the grass this way and that with its many stiff and shining legs. A frisky young Grasshopper kicked in the same way, and happened—just happened, of course—to knock over two of his friends. Then there was a great scrambling and the Crickets frolicked with them. The young Walking-Stick thought it looked like great fun and almost wished herself some other kind of insect, so that she could tumble around in the same way. She did not quite wish it, you understand, and would never have thought of it if she had turned brown.

"Ah," said the Five-

Legged Walking-Stick, "what scrambling! How very common!"

"Yes, indeed!" said his sister. "Why can't they learn to move slowly and gracefully? Perhaps they can't help being fat, but they might at least act genteel."

"What is it to be genteel?" asked a Grasshopper suddenly. He had heard every word that the Walking-Stick said.

"Why," said the Five-Legged Walking-Stick, "it is just to be genteel. To act as you see us act, and to—"

Just here the hay-tedder passed over them, and every one of the Walking-Sticks was sent flying through the air and landed on his back. The Grasshoppers declare that the Walking-Sticks tumbled and kicked and flopped around in a dreadfully common way until they were right side up. "Why," said the Measuring Worm, "you act like anybody else when the hay-tedder comes along!"

The Walking-Sticks looked very uncomfortable, and the brother and sister could not think of anything to say. It was the young green one who spoke at last. "I think," said she, "that it is much easier to act genteel when one is right side up."

THE DAY OF THE GREAT STORM

EVERYTHING in the meadow was dry and dusty. The leaves on the milkweeds were turning yellow with thirst, the field blossoms drooped their dainty heads in the sunshine, and the grass seemed to fairly rattle in the wind, it was so brown and dry.

All of the meadow people when they met each other would say, "Well, this *is* hot," and the Garter Snake, who had lived there longer than anyone else, declared that it was the hottest and driest time that he had ever known. "Really," he said, "it is so hot that I cannot eat, and such a thing never happened before."

The Grasshoppers and Locusts were very happy, for such weather was exactly what they liked. They didn't see how people could complain of such delightful scorching days. But that, you know, is always the way, for

everybody cannot be suited at once, and all kinds of weather are needed to make a good year.

The poor Tree Frog crawled into the coolest place he could find—hollow trees, shady nooks under the ferns, or even beneath the corner of a great stone. "Oh," said he, "I wish I were a Tadpole again, swimming in a shady pool. It is such a long, hot journey to the marsh that I cannot go. Last night I dreamed that I was a Tadpole, splashing in the water, and it was hard to awaken and find myself only an uncomfortable old Tree Frog."

Over his head the Katydids were singing, "Lovely weather! Lovely weather!" and the Tree Frog, who was a good-natured old fellow after all, winked his eye at them and said: "Sing away. This won't last always, and then it will be my turn to sing."

Sure enough, the very next day a tiny cloud drifted across the sky, and the Tree Frog, who always knew when the weather was about to change, began his rain-song. "Pukr-r-rup!" sang he, "Pukr-r-rup! It will rain! It will rain! R-r-r-rain!"

The little white cloud, grew bigger and blacker, and another came following after, then another, and another, and another, until the sky was quite covered with rushing black clouds. Then came a long, low rumble of thunder, and all the meadow people hurried to find shelter. The Moths and Butterflies hung on the under sides of great leaves. The Grasshoppers and their cousins crawled under burdock and mullein plants. The Ants scurried around to find their own homes. The Bees and Wasps, who had been gathering honey for their nests, flew swiftly back. Everyone was hurrying to be ready for the shower, and above all the rustle and stir could be heard the voice of the old Frog,

"Pukr-r-rup! Pukr-r-rup! It will rain! It will rain! R-r-r-rain!"

The wind blew harder and harder, the branches swayed and tossed, the leaves danced, and some even blew off of their mother trees; the hundreds of little clinging creatures clung more and more tightly to the leaves that sheltered them, and then the rain came, and such a rain! Great drops hurrying down from the sky, crowding each other, beating down the grass, flooding the homes of the Ants and Digger Wasps until they were half choked with water, knocking over the Grasshoppers and tumbling them about like leaves. The lightning flashed, and the thunder pealed, and often a tree would crash down in the forest near by when the wind blew a great blast.

When everybody was wet, and little rivulets of water were trickling through the grass and running into great puddles in the hollows, the rain stopped, stopped suddenly. One by one the meadow people crawled or swam into sight.

The Digger Wasp was floating on a leaf in a big puddle. He was too tired and wet to fly, and the whirling of the leaf made him feel sick and dizzy, but he stood firmly on his tiny boat and tried to look as though he enjoyed it.

The Ants were rushing around to put their homes in shape, the Spiders were busily eating their old webs, which had been broken and torn in the storm, and some were already beginning new ones. A large family of Bees, whose tree-home had been blown down, passed over the meadow in search for a new dwelling, and everybody seemed busy and happy in the cool air that followed the storm.

The Snake went gliding through the wet grass, as hungry as ever, the Tree Frog was as happy as when he was a Tadpole, and only the Grasshoppers and their cousins, the Locusts and Katydids, were cross. "Such a horrid rain!" they grumbled, "it spoiled all our fun. And after such lovely hot weather too."

"Now don't be silly," said the Tree Frog, who could be really severe when he thought best, "the Bees and the Ants are not complaining, and they had a good deal harder time than you. Can't you make the best of anything? A nice, hungry, cross lot you would be if it didn't rain, because then you would have no good, juicy food. It's better for you in the end as it is, but even if it were not, you might make the best of it as I did of the hot weather. When you have lived as long as I have, you will know that neither Grasshoppers nor Tree Frogs can have their way all the time, but that it always comes out all right in the end without their fretting about it."

THE STORY OF LILY PAD ISLAND

THIS is the story of a venturesome young Spider, who left his home in the meadow to seek his fortune in the great world.

He was a beautiful Spider, and belonged to one of the best families in the country around. He was a worker, too, for, as he had often said, there wasn't a lazy leg on his body, and he could spin the biggest, strongest, and shiniest web in the meadow. All the young people in the meadow liked him, and he was invited to every party, or dance, or picnic that they planned. If he had been content to stay at home, as his brothers and sisters were, he would in time have become as important and well known as the Tree Frog, or the fat, old Cricket, or even as the Garter Snake.

But that would not satisfy him at all, and one morning he said "Good-by" to all his friends and relatives, and set sail

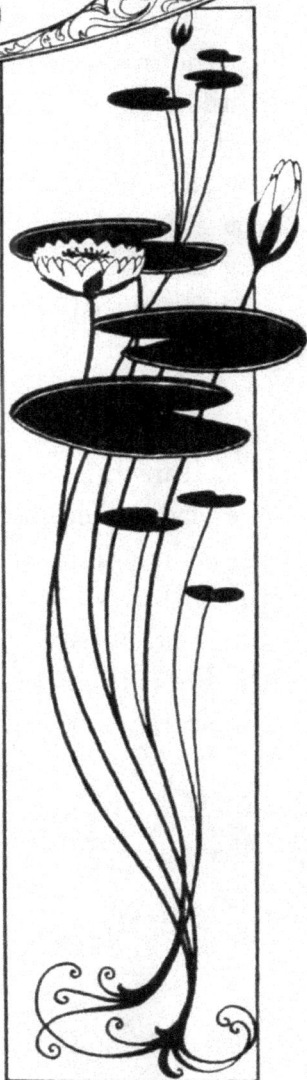

for unknown lands. He set sail, but not on water. He crawled up a tree, and out to the end of one of its branches. There he began spinning a long silken rope, and letting the wind blow it away from the tree. He held fast to one end, and when the wind was quite strong, he let go of the branch and sailed off through the air, carried by his rope balloon, and blown along by the wind.

The meadow people, on the ground below, watched him until he got so far away that he looked about as large as a Fly, and then he looked no bigger than an Ant, and then no bigger than a clover seed, and then no bigger than the tiniest egg that was ever laid, and then—well, then you could see nothing but sky, and the Spider was truly gone. The other young Spiders all wished that they had gone, and the old Spiders said, "They might much better stay at home, as their fathers and mothers had done." There was no use talking about it when they disagreed so, and very little more was said.

Meanwhile, the young traveller was having a very fine time. He was carried past trees and over fences, down toward the river. Under him were all the bright flowers of the meadow, and the bushes which used to tower above his head. After a while, he saw the rushes of the marsh below him, and wondered if the Frogs there would see him as he passed over them.

Next, he saw a beautiful, shining river, and in the quiet water by the shore were great white water-lilies growing, with their green leaves, or pads, floating beside them. "Ah," thought he, "I shall pass over the river, and land on the farther side," and he began to think of eating his rope balloon, so that he might

sink slowly to the ground, when—the wind suddenly stopped blowing, and he began falling slowly down, down, down, down.

How he longed for a branch to cling to! How he shivered at the thought of plunging into the cold water! How he wished that he had always stayed at home! How he thought of all the naughty things that he had ever done, and was sorry that he had done them! But it was of no use, for still he went down, down, down. He gave up all hope and tried to be brave, and at that very minute he felt himself alight on a great green lily-pad.

This was indeed an adventure, and he was very joyful for a little while. But he got hungry, and there was no food near. He walked all over the leaf, Lily-Pad Island he named it, and ran around its edges as many as forty times. It was just a flat, green island, and at one side was a perfect white lily, which had grown, so pure and beautiful, out of the darkness and slime of the river bottom. The lily was so near that he jumped over to it. There he nestled in its sweet, yellow centre, and went to sleep.

When he fell asleep it was late in the afternoon, and, as the sun sank lower and lower in the west, the lily began to close her petals and get ready for the night. She was just drawing under the water when the Spider awakened. It was dark and close, and he felt himself shut in and going down. He scrambled and pushed, and got out just in time to give a great leap and alight on Lily Pad-Island once more. And then he was in a sad plight. He was hungry and cold, and night was coming on, and, what was worst of all, in his great struggle to free himself from the lily he had pulled off two of his legs, so he had only six left.

He never liked to think of that night afterward, it was so dreadful. In the morning he saw a leaf come floating down the stream; he watched it; it touched Lily-Pad Island for just an instant and he jumped on. He did not know where it would take him, but anything was better than staying where he was and starving. It might float to the shore, or against one of the rushes that grew in the shallower parts of the river. If it did that, he would jump off and run up to the top and set sail again, but the island, where he had been, was too low to give him a start.

He went straight down-stream for a while, then the leaf drifted into a little eddy, and whirled around and around, until the Spider was almost too dizzy to stand on it. After that, it floated slowly, very slowly, toward the shore, and at last came the joyful minute when the Spider could jump to some of the plants that grew in the shallow water, and, by making rope bridges from one to another, get on solid ground.

After a few days' rest he started back to the meadow, asking his way of every insect that he met. When he got home they did not know him, he was so changed, but thought him only a tramp Spider, and not one of their own people. His mother was the first one to find out who he was, and when her friends said, "Just what I expected! He might have known better," she hushed them, and answered: "The poor child has had a hard time, and I won't scold him for going. He has learned that home is the best place, and that home friends are the dearest. I shall keep him quiet while his new legs are growing, and then, I think, he will spin his webs near the old place."

And so he did, and is now one of the steadiest of all the meadow people. When anybody asks him his age, he refuses to tell, "For," he says, "most of me is middle-aged, but these two new legs of mine are still very young."

THE GRASSHOPPER WHO WOULDN'T BE SCARED.

THERE were more Ants in the meadow than there were of any other kind of insects. In their family there were not only Ants, but great-aunts, cousins, nephews, and nieces, until it made one sleepy to think how many relatives each Ant had. Yet they were small people and never noisy, so perhaps the Grasshoppers seemed to be the largest family there.

There were many different families of Grasshoppers, but they were all related. Some had short horns, or feelers, and red legs; and some had long horns. Some lived in the lower part of the meadow where it was damp, and some in the upper part. The Katydids, who really belong to this family, you know, stayed in trees and did not often sing in the daytime. Then there were the great Road Grasshoppers who lived only in places where the ground was bare and dusty, and whom you could hardly see unless they were flying. When they lay in the dust their wide wings were hidden and they showed only that part of their bodies which was dust-color. Let the farmer drive along, however, and they rose into the air with a gentle, whirring sound and fluttered to a safe place. Then one could see them plainly, for their large under wings were black with yellow edges.

Perhaps those Grasshoppers who were best known in the meadow were the Clouded Grasshoppers, large dirty-brown ones with dark spots, who seemed to be everywhere during the autumn. The fathers and brothers in this family always crackled their wings loudly when they flew anywhere, so one could never forget that they were around.

It was queer that they were always spoken of as Grasshoppers. Their great-great-great-grandparents were called Locusts, and that was the family name, but the Cicadas liked that name and wanted it for themselves, and made such a fuss about it that people began to call them Seventeen-Year-Locusts; and then because they had to call the real Locusts something else, they called them Grasshoppers. The Grasshoppers didn't mind this. They were jolly and noisy, and as they grew older were sometimes very pompous. And you know what it is to be pompous.

When the farmer was drawing the last loads of hay to his barn and putting them away in the great mows there, three young Clouded Grasshopper brothers were frolicking near the wagon. They had tried to see who could run the fastest, crackle the loudest, spring the highest, flutter the farthest, and eat the most. There seemed to be nothing more to do. They couldn't eat another mouthful, the other fellows wouldn't play with them, they wouldn't play with their sisters, and they were not having any fun at all.

They were sitting on a hay-cock, watching the wagon as it came nearer and nearer. The farmer was on top and one of his men was walking beside it. Whenever they came to a hay-cock the farmer would stop the Horses, the man would run a long-handled, shining pitch-fork into the hay on the ground and throw it up to the farmer. Then it would be trampled down on to the load, the farmer's wife would rake up the scattering hay which was left on the ground, and that would be thrown up also.

The biggest Clouded Grasshopper said to his brothers, "You dare not sit still while they put this hay on the load!"

The smallest Clouded Grasshopper said, "I do too!"

The second brother said, "Huh! Guess I dare do anything you do!" He said it in a rather mean way, and that may have been because he had eaten too much. Overeating will make any insect cross.

Now every one of them was afraid, but each waited for the others to back out. While they were waiting, the wagon stopped beside them, the shining fork was run into the hay, and they were shaken and stood on their heads and lifted through the air on to the wagon. There they found themselves all tangled up with hay in the middle of the load. It was dark and they could hardly breathe. There were a few stems of nettles in the hay, and they had to crawl away from them. It was no fun at all, and they didn't talk very much.

When the wagon reached the barn, they were pitched into the mow with the hay, and then they hopped and fluttered around until they were on the floor over the Horses' stalls. They sat together on the floor and wondered how they could ever get back to the meadow. Because they had come in the middle of the load, they did not know the way.

"Oh!" said they. "Who are those four-legged people over there?"

"Kittens!" sang a Swallow over their heads. "Oh, tittle-ittle-ittle-ee!"

The Clouded Grasshoppers had

never seen Kittens. It is true that the old Cat often went hunting in the meadow, but that was at night, when Grasshoppers were asleep.

"Meouw!" said the Yellow Kitten. "Look at those queer little brown people on the floor. Let's each catch one."

So the Kittens began crawling slowly over the floor, keeping their bodies and tails low, and taking very short steps. Not one of them took his eyes off the Clouded Grasshopper whom he meant to catch. Sometimes they stopped and crouched and watched, then they went on, nearer, nearer, nearer, still, while the Clouded Grasshoppers were more and more scared and wished they had never left the meadow where they had been so safe and happy.

At last the Kittens jumped, coming down with their sharp little claws just where the Clouded Grasshoppers—had been. The Clouded Grasshoppers had jumped too, but they could not stay long in the air, and when they came down the Kittens jumped again. So it went until the poor Clouded Grasshoppers were very, very tired and could not jump half so far as they had done at first. Sometimes the Kittens even tried to catch them while they were fluttering, and each time they came a little nearer than before. They were so tired that they never thought of leaping up on the wall of the barn where the Kittens couldn't reach them.

At last the smallest Clouded Grasshopper called to his brothers, "Let us chase the Kittens."

The brothers answered, "They're too big."

The smallest Clouded Grasshopper, who had always been the brightest one in the family, called back, "We may scare them if they are big."

Then all the Clouded Grasshoppers leaped toward the Kittens and crackled their wings and looked very, very fierce. And the Kittens ran away as fast as they could. They were in such a hurry to get away that the Yellow Kitten tumbled over the White Kitten and they rolled on the floor in a furry little heap. The Clouded Grasshoppers leaped again, and the Kittens scrambled away to their nest in the hay, and stood against the wall and raised their backs and their pointed little tails, and opened their pink mouths and spat at them, and said, "Ha-ah-h-h!"

"There!" said the smallest Clouded Grasshopper to them, "we won't do anything to you this time, because you are young and don't know very much, but don't you ever bother one of us again. We might have hopped right on to you, and then what could you have done to help yourselves?"

The Clouded Grasshoppers started off to find their way back to the meadow, and the frightened Kittens looked at each other and whispered: "Just supposing they had hopped on to us! What *could* we have done!"

The Earthworm Half-Brothers

Early one wet morning, a long Earthworm came out of his burrow. He did not really leave it, but he dragged most of his body out, and let just the tip-end of it stay in the earth. Not having any eyes, he could not see the heavy, gray clouds that filled the sky, nor the milkweed stalks, so heavy with rain-drops that they drooped their pink heads. He could not see these things, but he could feel the soft, damp grass, and the cool, clear air, and as for seeing, why, Earthworms never do have eyes, and never think of wanting them, any more than you would want six legs, or feelers on your head.

This Earthworm had been out of his burrow only a little while, when there was a flutter and a rush, and Something flew down from the sky and bit his poor body in two. Oh, how it hurt! Both halves of him wriggled and twisted with pain, and there is no telling what might have become of them if another and bigger Something had not come rushing down to drive the first Something away. So there the poor Earthworm lay, in two aching, wriggling pieces, and although it had been easy enough to bite him in two, nothing in the world could ever bite him into one.

After a while the aching stopped, and he had time to think. It was very hard to decide what he ought to do. You can see just how puzzling it must have been, for, if you should suddenly find yourself two people instead of one, you would not know which one was which. At this very minute, who should come along but the Cicada, and one of the Earthworm pieces asked his advice. The Cicada thought that he was the very person to advise in such a case, because he had had such a puzzling time himself. So he said in a very knowing way: "Pooh! That is a simple matter. I thought I was two Cicadas once, but I wasn't. The thinking, moving part is the real one, whatever happens, so that part of the Worm which thinks and moves is the real Worm."

"I am the thinking part," cried each of the pieces.

The Cicada rubbed his head with his front legs, he was so surprised.

"And I am the moving part," cried each of the pieces, giving a little wriggle to prove it.

"Well, well, well, well!" exclaimed the Cicada, "I believe I don't know how to settle this. I will call the Garter Snake," and he flew off to get him.

A very queer couple they made, the Garter Snake and the Cicada, as they came hurrying back from the Snake's home. The Garter Snake was quite excited. "Such a thing has not happened in our meadow for a long time," he said, "and it is a good thing there is somebody here to explain it to you, or you would be dreadfully frightened. My family is related to the Worms, and I know. Both of you pieces are Worms

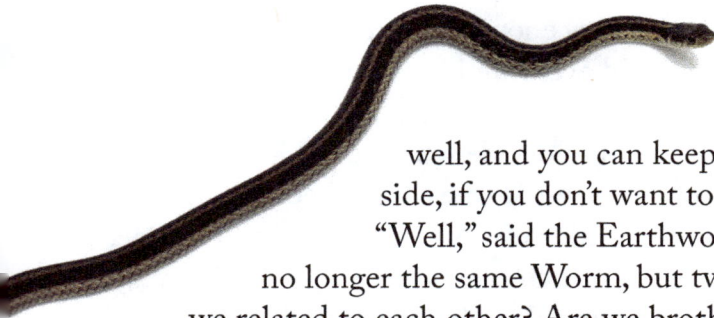

now. The bitten ends will soon be well, and you can keep house side by side, if you don't want to live together."

"Well," said the Earthworms, "if we are no longer the same Worm, but two Worms, are we related to each other? Are we brothers, or what?"

"Why," answered the Garter Snake, with a funny little smile, "I think you might call yourselves half-brothers." And to this day they are known as "the Earthworm half-brothers." They are very fond of each other and are always seen together.

A jolly young Grasshopper, who is a great eater and thinks rather too much about food, said he wouldn't mind being bitten into two Grasshoppers, if it would give him two stomachs and let him eat twice as much.

The Cicada told the Garter Snake this one day, and the Garter Snake said: "Tell him not to try it. The Earthworms are the only meadow people who can live after being bitten in two that way. The rest of us have to be one, or nothing. And as for having two stomachs, he is just as well off with one, for if he had two, he would get twice as hungry."

A GOSSIP-ING FLY

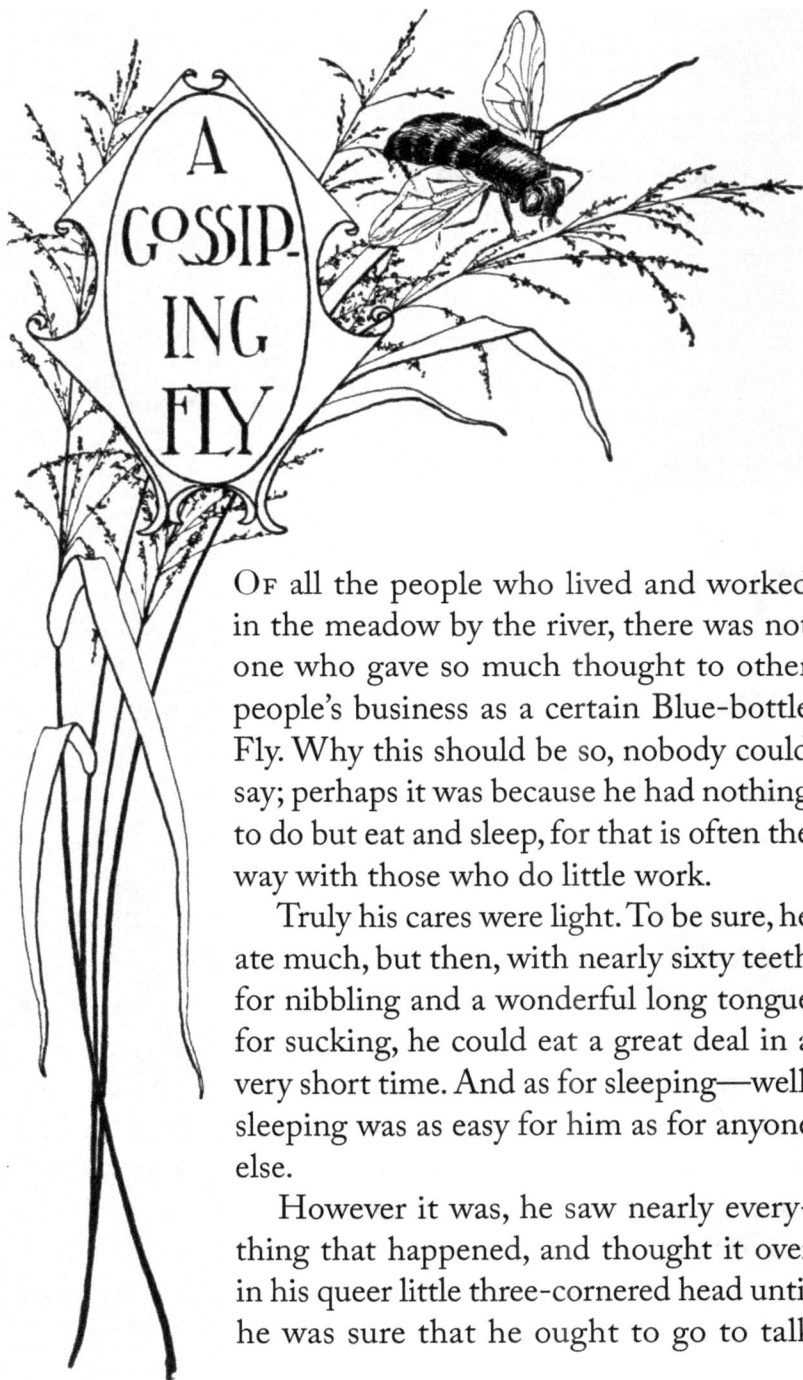

Of all the people who lived and worked in the meadow by the river, there was not one who gave so much thought to other people's business as a certain Blue-bottle Fly. Why this should be so, nobody could say; perhaps it was because he had nothing to do but eat and sleep, for that is often the way with those who do little work.

Truly his cares were light. To be sure, he ate much, but then, with nearly sixty teeth for nibbling and a wonderful long tongue for sucking, he could eat a great deal in a very short time. And as for sleeping—well, sleeping was as easy for him as for anyone else.

However it was, he saw nearly every-thing that happened, and thought it over in his queer little three-cornered head until he was sure that he ought to go to talk

about it with somebody else. It was
no wonder that he saw so much,
for he had a great bunch of eyes
on each side of his head, and three
bright, shining ones on the very
top of it. That let him see almost
everything at once,
and beside this his
neck was so exceed-
ingly slender that he could turn his
head very far around.

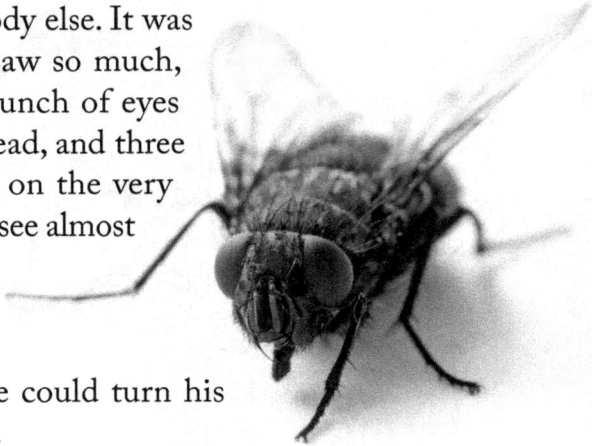

This particular Fly, like all other Flies,
was very fond of the sunshine and kept closely at home in
dark or wet weather. He had no house, but stayed in a certain
elder bush on cloudy days and called that his home. He had
spent all of one stormy day there, hanging on the under side
of a leaf, with nothing to do but think. Of course, his head
was down and his feet were up, but Blue-bottle Flies think in
that position as well as in any other, and the two sticky pads
on each side of his six feet held him there very comfortably.

He thought so much that day, that when the next morning dawned sunshiny and clear, he had any number of things
to tell people, and he started out at once.

First he went to the Tree Frog. "What do you suppose,"
said he, "that the Garter Snake is saying about you? It is
very absurd, yet I feel that you ought to know. He says that
your tongue is fastened at the wrong end, and that the tip
of it points down your throat. Of course, I knew it couldn't
be true, still I thought I would tell you what he said, and
then you could see him and put a stop to it."

For an answer to this the Tree Frog ran out his tongue, and, sure enough, it was fastened at the front end. "The Snake is quite right," he said pleasantly, "and my tongue suits me perfectly. It is just what I need for the kind of food I eat, and the best of all is that it never makes mischief between friends."

After that, the Fly could say nothing more there, so he flew away in his noisiest manner to find the Grasshopper who lost the race. "It was a shame," said the Fly to him, "that the judges did not give the race to you. The idea of that little green Measuring Worm coming in here, almost a stranger, and making so much trouble! I would have him driven out of the meadow, if I were you."

"Oh, that is all right," answered the Grasshopper, who was really a good fellow at heart; "I was very foolish about that race for a time, but the Measuring Worm and I are firm friends now. Are we not?" And he turned to a leaf just back of him, and there, peeping around the edge, was the Measuring Worm himself.

The Blue-bottle Fly left in a hurry, for where people were so good-natured he could do nothing at all. He went this time to the Crickets, whom he found all together by the fat, old Cricket's hole.

"I came," he said, "to find out if it were true, as the meadow people say, that you were all dreadfully frightened when the Cow came?"

The Crickets answered never a word, but they looked at each other and began asking him questions.

"Is it true," said one, "that you do nothing but eat and sleep?"

"Is it true," said another, "that your eyes are used most of the time for seeing other people's faults?"

"And is it true," said another, "that with all the fuss you make, you do little but mischief?"

The Blue-bottle Fly answered nothing, but started at once for his home in the elder bush, and they say that his three-cornered head was filled with very different thoughts from any that had been there before.

THE FROG-HOPPERS GO
OUT INTO THE WORLD.

ALONG the upper edge of the meadow and in the corners of the rail fence there grew golden-rod. During the spring and early summer you could hardly tell that it was there, unless you walked close to it and saw the slender and graceful stalks pushing upward through the tall grass and pointing in many different ways with their dainty leaves. The Horses and Cows knew it, and although they might eat all around it they never pulled at it with their lips or ate it. In the autumn, each stalk was crowned with sprays of tiny bright yellow blossoms, which nodded in the wind and scattered their golden pollen all around. Then it sometimes happened that people who were driving past would stop, climb over the fence, and pluck some of it to carry away. Even then there was so much left that one could hardly miss the stalks that were gone.

It may have been because the golden-rod was such a safe home that most of the Frog-Hoppers laid their eggs there. Some laid eggs in other plants and bushes, but most of them chose the golden-rod. After they had laid their eggs they wandered around on the grass, the bushes, and the few trees which grew in the meadow, hopping from one place to another and eating a little here and a little there.

Nobody knows why they should have been called Frog-Hoppers, unless it was because when you look them in the face they seem a very little like tiny Frogs. To be sure, they have six legs, and teeth on the front pair, as no real Frog ever thought of having. Perhaps it was only a nickname because their own name was so long and hard to speak.

The golden-rod was beginning to show small yellow-green buds on the tips of its stalks, and the little Frog-Hoppers were now old enough to talk and wonder about the great world. On one stalk four Frog-Hopper brothers and sisters lived close together. That was much pleasanter than having to grow up all alone, as most young Frog-Hoppers do, never seeing their fathers and mothers or knowing whether they ever would.

These four little Frog-Hoppers did not know how lucky they were, and that, you know, happens very often when people have not seen others lonely or unhappy. They supposed that every Frog-Hopper family had two brothers and two sisters living together on a golden-rod stalk. They fed on the juice or sap of the golden-rod, pumping it out of the stalk with their stout little beaks and eating or drinking it. After they had eaten it, they made white foam out of it, and this foam was all around them on the stalk. Any one passing by could tell at once by the foam just where the Frog-Hoppers lived.

One morning the oldest Frog-Hopper brother thought that the sap pumped very hard. It may be that it did pump hard, and it may be that he was tired or lazy. Anyway, he began to grumble

and find fault. "This is the worst stalk of golden-rod I ever saw in my life," he said. "It doesn't pay to try to pump any more sap, and I just won't try, so there!"

He was quite right in saying that it was the worst stalk he had ever seen, because he had never seen any other, but he was much mistaken in saying that it didn't pay to pump sap, and as for saying that "it didn't pay, so there!" we all know that when insects begin to talk in that way the best thing to do is to leave them quite alone until they are better-natured.

The other Frog-Hopper children couldn't leave him alone, because they hadn't changed their skins for the last time. They had to stay in their foam until that was done. After the big brother spoke in this way, they all began to wonder if the sap didn't pump hard. Before long the big sister wiggled impatiently and said, "My beak is dreadfully tired."

Then they all stopped eating and began to talk. They called their home stuffy, and said there wasn't room to turn around in it without hitting the foam. They didn't say why they should mind hitting the foam. It was soft and clean, and always opened up a way when they pushed against it.

"I tell you what!" said the big brother, "after I've changed my skin once more and gone out into the great world, you won't catch me hanging around this old golden-rod."

"Nor me!" "Nor me!" "Nor me!" said the other young Frog-Hoppers.

"I wonder what the world is like," said the little sister. "Is it just bigger foam and bigger golden-rod and more Frog-Hoppers?"

"Huh!" exclaimed her big brother. "What lots you know! If I didn't know any more than that about it, I'd keep still and not tell anybody." That made her feel badly, and she didn't speak again for a long time.

Then the little brother spoke. "I didn't know you had ever been out into the world," he said.

"No," said the big brother, "I suppose you didn't. There are lots of things you don't know." That made him feel badly, and he went off into the farthest corner of the foam and stuck his head in between a golden-rod leaf and the stalk. You see the big brother was very cross. Indeed, he was exceedingly cross.

For a long time nobody spoke, and then the big sister said, "I wish you would tell us what the world is like."

The big brother knew no more about the world than the other children, but after he had been cross and put on airs he didn't like to tell the truth. He might have known that he would be found out, yet he held up his head and answered: "I don't suppose that I can tell you so that you will understand, because you have never seen it. There are lots of things there—whole lots of them—and it is very big. Some of the things are like golden-rod and some of them are not. Some of them are not even like foam. And there are a great many people there. They all have six legs, but they are not so clever as we are. We shall have to tell them things."

This was very interesting and made the little sister forget to pout and the little brother come out of his foam-corner. He even looked as though he might ask a few questions, so the big brother added, "Now don't talk to me, for I must think about something."

It was not long after this that the young Frog-Hoppers changed their skins for the last time. The outside part of the foam hardened and made a little roof over them while they did this. Then they were ready to go out into the meadow. The big brother felt rather uncomfortable, and it was not his new skin which made him so. It was remembering what he had said about the world outside.

When they had left their foam and their golden-rod, they had much to see and ask about. Every little while one of the smaller Frog-Hoppers would exclaim, "Why, you never told us about this!" or, "Why didn't you tell us about that?"

Then the big brother would answer: "Yes, I did. That is one of the things which I said were not like either golden-rod or foam."

For a while they met only Crickets, Ants, Grasshoppers, and other six-legged people, and although they looked at each other they did not have much to say. At last they hopped near to the Tree Frog, who was sitting by the mossy trunk of a beech tree and looked so much like the bark that they did not notice him at first. The big brother was very near the Tree Frog's head.

"Oh, see!" cried the others. "There is somebody with only four legs, and he doesn't look as though he ever had any more. Why, Brother, what does this mean? You said everybody had six."

At this moment the Tree Frog opened his eyes a little and his mouth a great deal, and shot out his quick tongue. When he shut his mouth again, the big brother of the Frog-Hoppers was nowhere to be seen. They never had a chance to ask him that question again. If they had but known it, the Tree Frog at that minute had ten legs, for six and four are ten. But then, they couldn't know it, for six were on the inside.

THE MOSQUITO TRIES TO TEACH HIS NEIGHBORS

IN this meadow, as in every other meadow since the world began, there were some people who were always tired of the way things were, and thought that, if the world were only different, they would be perfectly happy. One of these discontented ones was a certain Mosquito, a fellow with a whining voice and disagreeable manners. He had very little patience with people who were not like him, and thought that the world would be a much pleasanter place if all the insects had been made Mosquitoes.

"What is the use of Spiders, and Dragon-flies, and Beetles, and Butter-flies?" he would say, fretfully; "a Mosquito is worth more than any of them."

You can just see how unreasonable he was. Of course, Mosquitoes and Flies do help keep the air pure

and sweet, but that is no reason why they should set themselves up above the other insects. Do not the Bees carry pollen from one flower to another, and so help the plants raise their Seed Babies? And who would not miss the bright, happy Butterflies, with their work of making the world beautiful?

But this Mosquito never thought of those things, and he said to himself: "Well, if they cannot all be Mosquitoes, they can at least try to live like them, and I think I will call them together and talk it over." So he sent word all around, and his friends and neighbors gathered to hear what he had to say.

"In the first place," he remarked, "it is unfortunate that you are not Mosquitoes, but, since you are not, one must make the best of it. There are some things, however, which you might learn from us fortunate creatures who are. For instance, notice the excellent habit of the Mosquitoes in the matter of laying eggs. Three or four hundred of the eggs are fastened together and left floating on a pond in such a way that, when the babies break their shells, they go head first into the water. Then they—"

"Do you think I would do that if I could?" interrupted a motherly old Grasshopper. "Fix it so my children would drown the minute they came out of the egg? No, indeed!"

and she hurried angrily away, followed by several other loving mothers.

"But they don't drown," exclaimed the Mosquito, in surprise.

"They don't if they're Mos-quitoes," replied the Ant, "but I am thankful to say my children are land babies and not water babies."

"Well, I won't say anything more about that, but I must speak of your voices, which are certainly too heavy and loud to be pleasant. I should think you might speak and sing more softly, even if you have no pockets under your wings like mine. I flutter my wings, and the air strikes these pockets and makes my sweet voice."

"Humph!" exclaimed a Bee, "it is a very poor place for pockets, and a very poor use to make of them. Every Bee knows that pockets are handiest on the hind legs, and should be used for carrying pollen to the babies at home."

"My pocket is behind," said a Spider, "and my web silk is kept there. I couldn't live without a pocket."

Some of the meadow people were getting angry, so the Garter Snake, who would always rather laugh than quarrel, glided forward and said: "My friends and neighbors; our speaker here has been so kind as to tell us how the

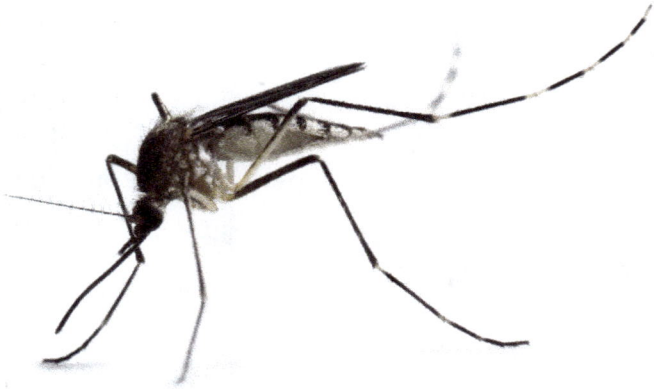

Mosquitoes do a great many things, and to try to teach us their way. It seems to me that we might repay some of his kindness by showing him our ways, and seeing that he learns by practice. I would ask the Spiders to take him with them and show him how to spin a web. Then the Bees could teach him how to build comb, and the Tree Frog how to croak, and the Earthworms how to burrow, and the Caterpillars how to spin a cocoon. Each of us will do something for him. Perhaps the Measuring Worm will teach him to walk as the Worms of his family do. I understand he does that very well." Here everybody laughed, remembering the joke played on the Caterpillars, and the Snake stopped speaking.

The Mosquito did not dare refuse to be taught, and so he was taken from one place to another, and told exactly how to do everything that he could not possibly do, until he felt so very meek and humble that he was willing the meadow people should be busy and happy in their own way.

THE FROG WHO THOUGHT HERSELF SICK

By the edge of the marsh lived a young Frog, who thought a great deal about herself and much less about other people. Not that it was wrong to think so much of herself, but it certainly was unfortunate that she should have so little time left in which to think of others and of the beautiful world.

Early in the morning this Frog would awaken and lean far over the edge of a pool to see how she looked after her night's rest. Then she would give a spring, and come down with a splash in the cool water for her morning bath. For a while she would swim as fast as her dainty webbed feet would push her, then she would rest, sitting in the soft mud with just her head above the water.

When her bath was taken, she had

her breakfast, and that was the way in which she began her day. She did nothing but bathe and eat and rest, from sunrise to sunset. She had a fine, strong body, and had never an ache or a pain, but one day she got to thinking, "What if sometime I should be sick?" And then, because she thought about nothing but her own self, she was soon saying, "I am afraid I shall be sick." In a little while longer it was, "I certainly am sick."

She crawled under a big toadstool, and sat there looking very glum indeed, until a Cicada came along. She told the Cicada how sick she felt, and he told his cousins, the Locusts, and they told their cousins, the Grasshoppers, and they told their cousins, the Katydids, and then everybody told somebody else, and started for the toadstool where the young Frog sat. The more she had thought of it, the worse she felt, until, by the time the meadow people came crowding around, she was feeling very sick indeed.

"Where do you feel badly?" they cried, and, "How long have you been sick?" and one Cricket stared with big eyes, and said, "How dr-r-readfully she looks!" The young Frog felt weaker and weaker, and answered in a faint little voice that she had felt perfectly well until after breakfast, but that now she was quite sure her skin was getting dry, and "Oh dear!" and "Oh dear!"

Now everybody knows that Frogs breathe through their skins as well as through their

noses, and for a Frog's skin to get dry is very serious, for then he cannot breathe through it; so, as soon as she said that, everybody was frightened and wanted to do something for her at once. Some of the timid ones began to weep, and the others bustled around, getting in each other's way and all trying to do something different. One wanted to wrap her in mullein leaves, another wanted her to nibble a bit of the peppermint which grew near, a third thought she should be kept moving, and that was the way it went.

Just when everybody was at his wits' end, the old Tree Frog came along. "Pukr-r-rup! What is the matter with you?" he said.

"Oh!" gasped the young Frog, weakly, "I am sure my skin is getting dry, and I feel as though I had something in my head."

"Umph!" grunted the Tree Frog to himself, "I guess there isn't enough in her head to ever make her sick; and, as for her skin, it isn't dry yet, and nobody knows that it ever will be."

But as he was a wise old fellow and had learned much about life, he knew he must not say such things aloud. What he did say was, "I heard there was to be a great race in the pool this morning."

The young Frog lifted her head quite quickly, saying: "You did? Who are the racers?"

"Why, all the young Frogs who live around here. It is too bad that you cannot go."

"I don't believe it would hurt me any," she said.

"You might take cold," the Tree Frog said; "besides, the exercise would tire you."

"Oh, but I am feeling much better," the young Frog said, "and I am certain it will do me good."

"You ought not to go," insisted all the older meadow people. "You really ought not."

"I don't care," she answered, "I am going anyway, and I am just as well as anybody."

And she did go, and it did seem that she was as strong as ever. The people all wondered at it, but the Tree Frog winked his eyes at them and said, "I knew that it would cure her." And then he, and the Garter Snake, and the fat, old Cricket laughed together, and all the younger meadow people wondered at what they were laughing.

THE KATYDIDS' QUARREL

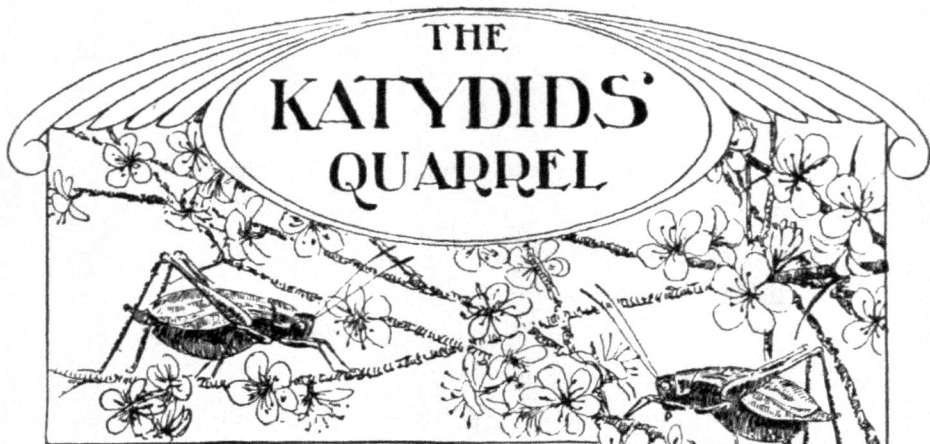

THE warm summer days were past, and the Katydids came again to the meadow. Everybody was glad to see them, and the Grasshoppers, who are cousins of the Katydids, gave a party in their honor.

Such a time as the meadow people had getting ready for that party! They did not have to change their dresses, but they scraped and cleaned themselves, and all the young Grasshoppers went off by the woods to practise jumping and get their knees well limbered, because there might be games and dancing at the party, and then how dreadful it would be if any young Grasshopper should find that two or three of his legs wouldn't bend easily!

The Grasshoppers did not know at just what time they ought to have the party. Some of the meadow people whom they wanted to invite were used

to sleeping all day, and some were used to sleeping all night, so it really was hard to find an hour at which all would be wide-awake and ready for fun. At last the Tree Frog said: "Pukr-r-rup! Pukr-r-rup! Have it at sunset!" And at sunset it was.

Everyone came on time, and they hopped and chattered and danced and ate a party supper of tender green leaves. Some of the little Grasshoppers grew sleepy and crawled among the plantains for a nap. Just then a big Katydid said he would sing a song—which was a very kind thing for him to do, because he really did it to make the others happy, and not to show what a fine musician he was. All the guests said, "How charming!" or, "We should be delighted!" and he seated himself on a low swinging branch. You know Katydids sing with the covers of their wings, and so when he alighted on the branch he smoothed down his pale green suit and rubbed his wing-cases a little to make sure that they were in tune. Then he began loud and clear, "Katy did! Katy did!! Katy did!!!"

Of course he didn't mean any real Katy, but was just singing his song. However, there was another Katydid there

who had a habit of contradicting, and he had eaten too much supper, and that made him feel crosser than ever; so when the singer said "Katy did!" this cross fellow jumped up and said, "Katy didn't! Katy didn't!! Katy didn't!!!" and they kept at it, one saying that she did and the other that she didn't, until everybody was ashamed and uncomfortable, and some of the little Grasshoppers awakened and wanted to know what was the matter.

Both of the singers got more and more vexed until at last neither one knew just what he was saying—and that, you know, is what almost always happens when people grow angry. They just kept saying something as loud and fast as possible and thought all the while that they were very bright—which was all they knew about it.

Suddenly somebody noticed that the one who began to say "Katy did!" was screaming "Katy didn't!" and the one who had said "Katy didn't!" was roaring "Katy did!" Then they all laughed, and the two on the branch looked at each other in a very shamefaced way.

The Tree Frog always knew the right thing to do, and he said "Pukr-r-rup!" so loudly that all stopped talking at once. When they were quiet he said: "We will now listen to a duet, 'Katy,' by the two singers who are up the tree. All please join in the chorus." So it was begun again, and both the leaders were good-natured, and all the Katydids below joined in with "did or didn't, did or didn't, did or didn't." And that was the end of the quarrel.

THE LAST PARTY OF THE SEASON

SUMMER had been a joyful time in the meadow. It had been a busy time, too, and from morning till night the chirping and humming of the happy people there had mingled with the rustle of the leaves, and the soft "swish, swish," of the tall grass, as the wind passed over it.

True, there had been a few quarrels, and some unpleasant things to remember, but these little people were wise enough to throw away all the sad memories and keep only the glad ones. And now the summer was over. The leaves of the forest trees were turning from green to scarlet, orange, and brown. The beech and hickory nuts were only waiting for a friendly frost to open their outer shells, and loosen their stems, so that they could fall to the earth.

The wind was cold now, and the meadow people knew that the time had come to get ready for winter. One chilly Caterpillar said to another, "Boo-oo! How cold it is! I must find a place for my cocoon. Suppose we sleep side by side this winter, swinging on the same bush?"

And his friend replied: "We must hurry then, or we shall be too old and stiff to spin good ones."

The Garter Snake felt sleepy all the time, and declared that in a few days he would doze off until spring.

The Tree Frog had chosen his winter home already, and the Bees were making the most of their time in visiting the last fall flowers, and gathering every bit of honey they could find for their cold-weather stock.

The last eggs had been laid, and the food had been placed beside many of them for the babies that would hatch out in the spring. Nothing was left but to say "Good-by," and fall asleep. So a message was sent around the meadow for all to come to a farewell party under the elm tree.

Everybody came, and all who could sing did so, and the Crickets and Mosquitoes made music for the rest to dance by.

The Tree Frog led off with a black and yellow Spider, the Garter Snake followed with a Potato Bug, and all the other crawling people joined in the dance on the grass, while over their heads the Butterflies and other light-winged ones fluttered to and fro with airy grace.

The Snail and the fat, old Cricket had meant to look on, and really did so, for a time, from a warm corner by the tree, but the Cricket couldn't stand it to not join in the fun. First, his eyes gleamed, his feelers waved, and his feet kept time to the music, and, when a frisky young Ant beckoned to him, he gave a great leap and danced with the rest, balancing, jumping, and circling around in a most surprising way.

When it grew dark, the Fireflies' lights shone like tiny stars, and the dancing went on until all were tired and ready to sing together the last song of the summer, for on the morrow they would go to rest. And this was their song:

> The autumn leaves lying
>   So thick on the ground,
> The summer Birds flying
>   The meadow around,
>   Say, "Good-by."
>
> The Seed Babies dropping
>   Down out of our sight,
> The Dragon-flies stopping
>   A moment in flight,
>   Say, "Good-by."
>
> The red Squirrels bearing
>   Their nuts to the tree,
> The wild Rabbits caring
>   For babies so wee,
>   Say, "Good-by."
>
> The sunbeams now showing
>   Are hazy and pale,
> The warm breezes blowing
>   Have changed to a gale,
>   So, "Good-by."

The season for working
   Is passing away.
Both playing and shirking
   Are ended to day,
      So, "Good-by."

The Garter Snake creeping
   So softly to rest,
The fuzzy Worms sleeping
   Within their warm nest,
      Say, "Good-by."

The Honey Bees crawling
   Around the full comb,
The tiny Ants calling
   Each one to the home,
      Say, "Good-by."

We've ended our singing,
   Our dancing, and play,
And Nature's voice ringing
   Now tells us to say
      Our "Good-by."